BROKEN T

BROKEN TIME
The Complete Script

Mick Martin

Scratching Shed Publishing Ltd

Back cover : Original cast members Emily Butterfield,
Andy Cresswell, Anthony Hunt, Andrew Price, Gareth
Richards, Mike Hugo and Howard Chadwick.
Photographer: Dave Lynch

A catalogue record for this book is available from the
British Library.

Typeset in Warnock Pro Semi Bold and Palatino
Printed and bound in the United Kingdom by
Charlesworth Press, Flanshaw Way, Flanshaw Lane,
Wakefield, WF2 9LP

Original Cast

Lewy Jenkins	Gareth Richards
Herbert Dalton	Howard Chadwick
Rev Marshall	Andy Price
Bessie Butterworth	Emily Butterfield
Gil Gannon	Anthony Hunt
Annie Wilkinson	Susie Emmett
George Wilkinson	Andy Cresswell
Harry Stockwell	Michael Hugo

Director	Conrad Nelson
Producers	Greg Boardman
	Jude Wright
Executive Producers	Nick Dhandsa
	Eugenio Perez

Broken Time was produced by Three Stones Media and premiered at Wakefield Theatre Royal on Wednesday 21 September 2011, supported by the National Lottery through Arts Council England.

The production was designed by Barney George, choreographed by Adam Sunderland and musically directed by Rebecca Hughes.

Introduction

Rugby: The Class Game

By Professor Tony Collins
Director, International Centre for Sports History and
Culture, De Montfort University, Leicester

The Victorians were obsessed with class. They analysed the tiny gradations of social distinction with painstaking detail. Variations in accent, manners and clothes were studied with the intensity of Charles Darwin examining the creatures of the Galapagos islands.

Their greatest fear was that the ornate hierarchy of the British class system would be undermined. Thomas Hardy's *Jude the Obscure*, published in 1895, tells the sorry and ultimately tragic tale of a stonemason who has ideas above his station and yearns to go to university.

More alarmingly, H.G. Wells' *The Time Machine*, which also appeared in 1895, portrayed a future in which the industrial working-class had become a different human species, the Morlocks, who hunt and eat the leisured descendants of the upper classes.

This deep anxiety about class was seen not only in the drawing rooms and boardrooms of well-to-do Victorians. As *Broken Time* so brilliantly depicts, it was also fought out with brutal intensity on the rugby pitch in the 1880s and 1890s.

For the men who led rugby, educated at public and grammar schools and proud of their middle-class heritage, the game's massive popularity in the industrial towns and cities of the north filled them with dread.

They had seen how soccer quickly became dominated by the working class after the FA legalised professionalism in 1885 - and they did not like it. 'No mercy but iron rigour will be dealt out' to working-class professionals, declared RFU president Arthur Budd.

They were not alone. Fear of the working class grew rapidly in the 1880s. In 1886 and 1887 Trafalgar Square saw two major riots over unemployment and oppression in Ireland. These were followed by major strikes by match-girls, dockers and gas workers in the late 1880s which inspired the growth of the militant 'new union' movement.

In the north, social tensions became far more acute. In 1890, cavalry attacked a demonstration supporting striking Leeds gas workers. Later that year over 5,000 men and women went on strike for almost five months at Manningham Mills in Bradford. In 1892 cotton manufacturers in Lancashire locked out their workers.

Class conflict reached its peak in 1893. In Hull, striking dockers were confronted by naval gunboats in the Humber. In Featherstone, the army was called out to oppose striking miners - troops shot two dead and wounded sixteen others in an attempt to 'restore law and order'

For the upper and middle classes, old certainties were disappearing and dread of the power of the working class was rising. 'Our civilisation is nothing but a thin film or crust lying over a volcanic pit...[it is to be wondered] whether some day the pit would not break up through it and destroy us all,' the novelist Mark Rutherford speculated fearfully.

This was the backdrop to the story that *Broken Time* presents. It may be a work of fiction, but it is a play that illuminates a great truth.

In 1886 the Rugby Football Union (RFU), the game's governing body, decided to act against the growing influence of the working class on the game. It banned all forms of payment to players and officially made the game amateur. Then it began a witch hunt to root out the 'veiled professional', suspending players and clubs. Players were even investigated for receiving wedding presents from supporters.

Even so, this did nothing to stop the advance of working-class teams in the north. The county championship was won by Yorkshire every year except one. That was in 1891, when the title was won by the equally proletarian Lancashire side.

Even the national side was slipping out of control. Eleven of the English fifteen that defeated Scotland in 1892 were from Lancashire and Yorkshire - and ten of those were manual workers.

This was not a north versus south divide but a class issue, as Yorkshire cricket and rugby international Frank Mitchell made clear: 'The Rugby game, as its name implies, sprang from our public schools. It has been developed by our leading London clubs and universities; and why should we hand it over without a struggle to the hordes of working men players who would quickly engulf all others?'

Broken Time

The RFU's attitude to working-class players and spectators combined disdain with dread. When the leading northern clubs suggested allowing players to receive 'broken-time' payments for time taken off work to play rugby in the autumn of 1893, the RFU drew a line in the sand.

Once the RFU had rejected the broken-time proposal, it started to suspend northern teams. Huddersfield were first to feel its wrath. In Lancashire, Leigh, Salford and Wigan were suspended and others under investigation. It was clear that the RFU wanted to drive the northern clubs out of rugby.

Faced with the choice of surrender or split, the leading northern clubs met at the George Hotel in Huddersfield on 29 December 1895. They voted to leave the RFU and form a new Northern Rugby Football Union, which immediately legalised broken-time payments.

Rugby would never be the same.

Within a few years the Northern Union had reduced the players in a team to thirteen, increased the value of try-scoring over goal-kicking and replaced the ruck and the maul with the play-the-ball. The new sport of rugby league had emerged.

But the social divisions remained. The RFU banned for life anyone who played rugby league, whether amateur or professional. Even meeting with rugby league club officials was punished by a life ban from the union game.

Wherever in the world rugby was played, the same prejudices dominated. When the British rugby union teamed toured New Zealand in 1930, their manager was asked why rugby league was so popular in Auckland. 'Every town must have its sewer,' he replied contemptuously.

It was a system described approvingly by South African rugby president Danie Craven 'as the strictest form of apartheid'. It lasted until 1995 when, almost one hundred years to the day after rugby's great split, rugby union decided to abandon its amateur principles and become a professional game.

Today, the cultural gulf between league and union still persists. A visit to Castleford's Wheldon Road stadium is a very different experience to a trip to Leicester's Welford Road ground.

Much has changed in sport and British society since 1895, but rugby is a still a microcosm of British society. And the obsession with class remains as strong as ever.

Tony Collins,
September 2013

Foreword

By Mick Martin

L ike most rugby league supporters, I had a vague notion about how the game came to be - the Northern Union breaking away at the George Hotel in Huddersfield in 1890-odd. So when Greg Boardman of Three Stones Media asked me to write a play about it, I was more than happy.

What I discovered is a history that is not just rich and complex, but also linked into the social and political history of the times in a profound way. The birth of the Northern Union, and thus rugby league, is inextricably linked with the emancipation of the working class, with the social and political history of this country.

Researching the play has made a lot of things I'd always taken for granted about the game make sense. Things like why the 'heartlands' are the heartlands, and the real and profound reasons why it's the working class game while the other code is the middle/upper class one.

Rugby league has come to be known as the people's game, but in the 1800s there were working men and women as passionately obsessed with what was then just 'rugby' as anyone today. It pulled huge crowds, and as the Yorkshire and Lancashire teams, increasingly made up of working men, came to dominate the game, it became a symbol of the social and political upheaval that was gathering pace in the country at large. Something had to give.

The events leading up to the historic moment at the George Hotel in 1895 have been documented superbly by Tony Collins. I am deeply indebted to him and without his work on the subject I would have struggled to write this play. I cannot compete with him for academic detail, but the thing a play can add to the discussion, the understanding of the subject, lies in the way it permits us to explore characters, investigate the motives and underlying intentions of all involved, in a more focussed, accessible and entertaining fashion. It brings the key players to life, warts and all, and places the men and women of those times before us as real flesh and blood characters, with voices, humour, feelings and failings.

The issues and motivations at the heart of *Broken Time*, a battle royal for the very soul of a game, more than that, for the desire of an entire class to have a say in its own destiny, lend themselves to a drama more readily than most.

At the centre of the story is Reverend Frank "bell book and candle" Marshall, known as "the scourge of professionalism". He is a real historical figure who was so central to the arguments, so passionately opposed to professionalism in any form, that he had to be in the play.

The remaining characters are fictional however. In

some cases they are an amalgamation of several real, historical figures, brought under one hat as it were, to represent one particular strand of argument within the story.

The reason for this is so that events and argument that were spread out over a lengthy period of time, and geography, could be brought into one location, the town and rugby club of West Broughton, owned by the local mill owner Herbert Dalton. It centres on his decision to bring a Welsh player to the club in a bid to boost the team's performance. The arrival in West Broughton of Lewy Jenkins, the David Beckham of his day, lights the spark that puts Reverend Marshall and Herbert Dalton on collision course.

The play seeks to explore fully the world of northern rugby, and the pressures on all involved in the game, in the years leading up to the great schism.

Ultimately the split had as much to do with club owners, the wealthy entrepreneurs of the day, and their desire to control their clubs and run them along lines business lines that they were more accustomed to, as it had to do with working players expressing their desire to be paid for 'broken time' at work. It is about the very birth of professional sport. The arguments within it, about money, class and power are as relevant to us now as they were in 1895.

Ironically, some of Reverend Marshall's arguments about professionalism, how it will create mercenaries out of sportsmen, have not exactly proved groundless in the century and a bit since. But the times were changing all around him and the momentum towards the break was gathering pace. It is a story that involved real people, and lives that were transformed and in some cases trampled along the way.

I am really indebted to Greg Boardman of Three Stones Media for all his input, support and enthusiasm along the way, to Tony Collins for his depth of knowledge on the

Broken Time

subject, to Mike Stephenson for his passionate support and
advocacy throughout the project and lastly to Conrad Nelson,
the director, and all the actors who helped make such a fine
production.

Rugby league is a great game, part of our cultural
fabric and shared history. I hope I've done its incredible story
justice.

Mick Martin
September, 2013.

Broken Time

by

Mick Martin

FIRST HALF

SCENE 1
The sound of the mill hooter. A sign reads **West Broughton versus Brighouse today kick off 3pm, February 15th, 1893**.

Lads with rugby boots appear, all running from the mill to the field. One of them is **Gil Gannon**. Enter **George Wilkinson**, he rushes Gil and rugby tackles him from behind. Gil is knocked flying.

George	Got you! Eh up Gilbert me old cock sparrow!
Gil	Gerroff me you sackless twonk!
George	Just practising me tackle technique.
Gil	Go out in yon field and practice on an old bullock instead of me! I've worked all morning, now I've a game to ready myself for, if I aren't on crutches after you've clattered me.
George	Take more than that to put you on crutches ar Gil. You made o' steel man! Oh breathe that in!
Gil	Breathe what in, what've you done?
George	Saturday! I love it! It's like... there's something about it... in the air... everything just feels different. You can smell it!
Gil	(*breathes in*) All I can whiff is fags and pies, stale pale ale, the Friday night philanderin'

of a small industrial town and… what's this… (*produces a small bottle*) and old Ma Blenkinsop's muscle rub for the relief of aches, pains and other unwanted bodily sensations, here have some!

He offers a bottle of the cure-all to George who gladly accepts, and swigs it.

George   Urgghh bugger me that's strong wallop is that!

Gil   Muscle *rub*, lame brain! You don't swallow it!

George   It's not too bad actually.

He has another swig, then sharply shoves the bottle to Gil on sight of his wife **Annie**, she is pregnant. She goes to George.

George   Oh nallacks, it's our Annie!

Annie   Gil. George.

Gil   Hello Annie.

Annie   (*to George*) Now, straight home wi' your money this week, and I mean our home, not the Bridge Hotel!

George   I know where I live Annie!

Annie   And not the flamin bookie's either!

George   Alright, bloody hell!

Annie	And come here while I attle you together, look at state of you, anybody'd think you kipped in't street.

She commences 'attling' him together – ie buttoning up his shirt, doing his collar, wetting her hand and rubbing it over his hair to smooth it etc.

Gil	He many a time does, few pints on him.
Annie	Gil.
Gil	Annie?
Annie	Button it, before I button it for you. And you know what I think about drinking as well, when the beer's in…
George	The sense is out, yes I know, will you leave us be!
Annie	I am not having you getting changed wi' all them gents looking like somat off a mill floor.
Gil	He won't be getting changed wi' all them gents, they have their own private facility a don't you know.
Annie	It's none of our business what they have, they have what's theirs and we stick to what's ours, show 'em proper respect, do unto others, speak when you're spoken to and not otherwise.
George	Aye, you wouldn't like it in there though Gil, can't even fart.

Gil   The expulsion of rancid foul air through the
        backside as the ultimate expression of the
        working man's identity... discuss.

She smiles at George, full of pride and love in her eyes.

Annie   Ah, that's better. Now, be sure and give 'em
        some proper panhandle! Knees and elbows!
        And tackle 'em low! For wi'out their legs
        they cannot go!

George Alright alright, I know I know!

Annie   I know you know... I just like telling you
        again cos I'm excited! Right I'm off, see you's
        after! Have 'em!!

Annie goes. Gil grins at George.

Gil   The words tiger by the tail come to mind.
        Did she never play rugby?

George Be no-one safe if Annie got on't field. Do you
        reckon it'll rain this aft?

Gil   Hope not, that rec turns into a bog in't
        slingin' it down.

George No bother to me ain't that, I'll skim straight
        over't puddles and under't posts.

Gil   Walkin' on water? You want be careful. Last
        bloke to try that made enemies.

George Really? Who'd he play for?

They catch each other's eye, then both crack out laughing. Up comes a local news reporter.

Wagstaff   Gil, George,

Gil/ George   Mr Wagstaff.

Wagstaff   Looking forward to a good game today boys, any words for the Yorkshireman?

Gil   Yes the days of international capitalism are numbered and the workers…

Wagstaff   Regarding the game Gil!

Gil   Oh. There's a big fat bastard called Eckersley, plays for Brighouse, and I look forward to crunching his…

Wagstaff   That I can print! George?

George   Err… erm… All the boys…

Gil   And gentlemen.

Wagstaff scribbles busily as George thinks deeply about each word before he says it. Gil and Wagstaff look on blankly.

George   Are right set to… stop larking about… like big Aunt Jesse's… on a church day out… to Knaresborough… and… er… start knocking the pasty out of 'em right and proper like we were at start o't season, aye!

Wagstaff	(*scribbling*) Ready to consign our recent run of indifferent form to the history books and return to winnings ways.
George	Did I say that? I didn't say that… did I?
Wagstaff	Now to what do you ascribe the recent deterioration in performance levels?
George	The what?
Gil	How come we're so crap?
George	Well I wouldn't right like to say…
Gil	I would, too many toffee nosed gents not enough proper panhandlers in't team. (*pause*) it's alright 'em complaining about us working lads, but it's us who gets stuck in, at the sharp end, where it hurts, at play and work just the…
Wagstaff	Thanks Gil I get the message! Have a good game lads!
Gil/George	Mr Wagstaff.

Wagstaff moves off but then takes his pad and pen and starts to scribble further as the scene continues.

Gil	Just think, tomorrow morning, there'll be folk, young and old, rich and poor… reading your words of wisdom.
George	(*beaming*) Aye. Says George Wilkinson, the West Broughton flyer!

Gil	Irony being you won't be able to join 'em. Annie'll read it out to you don't worry.
George	(*hurt*) You shouldn't take the mick like that.
Gil	I asked you to come to our Sunday school classes, but you had other things to do. Judging by't state of Annie, I'd say you did 'em.
George	Maybe if you spent a bit less time on meetings and spoutin' you might be courting yourself, have you thought of that?
Gil	No. I am married… and faithful… to the union.

A gentleman player approaches.

Gent	Hello George, Gil, a very good afternoon to you both.
Gil	(*mimicking*) Yes and the same to you old bean.
Gent	I appreciate that was an attempt at wit and shan't embarrass you by stating quite how badly it failed.
Gil	And I won't embarrass you by reminding you that rugby's about tackling, not tickling.
George	Gil! (*to the gent*) Hello Mr Frobisher, ignore him, how's your Gert and the bairn farin'?

Gent	I beg your pardon?
Gil	My colleague is merely enquiring after the wellbeing of your good lady wife and child.
Gent	Both are quite well, thankyou.
Gil	(*to George*) He says gert an' bairn are...
George	(*in*) I heard thanks very much! Oh that's good. Only my gert's banna pop any day like, aye, what say you and your... er... good lady wife, bring your babby round to ours and they can lake out together?
Gil	Aye, go rattin' and that... what do you think?
Gent	(*baffled*) Er... yes... of course.
George	(*grins*) Smashing. Annie'll be tickled pink.
Gent	Well, do excuse me, I shall see you both out on the field in a little while, let's hope we win for a change eh?
George	Let's hope so Mr Frobisher.

The gent departs, Gil looks at him in disbelief.

Gil	Oh, look George!
George	What?
Gil	See it, a big fat pink arse with a little curly tail... just flew over't top o't stand. Like he's

	gonna bring that little un anywhere near yours!
George	How do you know? You talk too sharp sometimes Gil. You could start a brawl in empty midden. I think it'd be nice for 'em to lake together.
Gil	Come on, let's go play some rugby.
George	Aye. Win today and there'll be a nice few bob in us boots after't match eh… leg of lamb dropped round house for Sunday dinner.
Gil	And if we lose, fourpence and dry bread.
George	So what? I love playing for West Broughton… it's all I dreamt of as a kid… running out… hearin't crowd… scorin' tries… there's no putting a price on that.

Across the stage Wagstaff looks up from his pad, reads what he has written.

| Wagstaff | So… the game is essentially dependent on working men, we should be careful not to depopularize the game and make it the selfish provision of the silver spooned classes… Moreover, it would deprive the pastime of it's ablest and most numerous exponents, who are essentially the working men of the north, and of its most enthusiastic supporters, who are undoubtedly the wage earning classes. |

Wagstaff is chipper with his article, puts his pad and pen away and departs. The band plays as the atmosphere of the match builds up.

SCENE 2

The main stand. Enter Harry Stockwell, followed by a reluctant Bessie Butterworth.

Bessie	If it rains I'm going straight home! Why do I even have to come anyway? There's nothing bores my cream sundaes off more than football!
Harry	Because, sweet cherub, I need to make friends and influence people in this town, and the kind of people I need to make friends and influence not only own rugby clubs and run mills, but are partial to the society of a comely female! And since I couldn't find one of them, you're here.
Bessie	(*mock laughter*) Just remember your promise! You said we wouldn't even be in this dump more than a year, you said you'd get me on at Leicester Square!
Harry	And I will, I've written to impresarios in London, and sent your photographs off, don't worry the ones with the frock on.
Bessie	You're all heart Harry Stockwell.
Harry	I am but keep that to yourself, I don't want folk getting the wrong impression. Now

straighten your frock, shut your gob and smile.

Bessie   ow do I shut my gob *and* smile? On second thoughts don't answer that! I don't know why I put up with you.

Harry   Because, deep down, you love me.

Bessie's look suggests otherwise. Enter Herbert Dalton.

Herbert   Good afternoon Harry.

Harry   Mr Dalton, what a pleasure sir, truly it be, may I introduce my acquaintance, Miss Bessie Butterworth, ascending star of the music hall stage.

Herbert   (*smitten*) Miss Butterworth.

Bessie   (*sweet*) Mr Dalton.

Herbert   Bessie.

Bessie   (*pause*) Golly, I'm all a flutter.

Herbert   Oh you needn't be, come, join me, in the stand.

Bessie   Thankyou so much. Harry tells me you're... big in the textiles hereabouts?

Herbert   Big, Miss Butterworth, is way too *small* a word for what I am hereabouts... every brick, cobble and ginnel for miles around either me or my dear old father put 'em there, the biggest house in Yorkshire, the tallest chimney in the north, the longest weaving shed in the world, until old Sir Titus went and outdid us at Salts Mill, God rest him! Big, Miss Butterworth, why they even call me Mr West Broughton and do you know why…

Bessie   Because you're cold, dirty and 10 years out of date?

Harry   (*mock laughter/mortified*) Aha! As you can see Miss Butterworth has er… spirit, she is after all a *music hall turn* so… the boundary twixt stage banter and polite proper conversation occasionally eludes her!

Herbert   No it doesn't, she speaks her mind. She's no fool. I like her.

Bessie smiles, mock sweet and gives Harry a dirty look to boot.

Harry   And the wool trade Mr Dalton? Are you still foraging gamely ahead, leading the world? A licence to print your own five pound notes?

Herbert   It's on it bloody knees. Worse than for many a year. Big storms a brewing… seen it with that strike at Manningham already, add to that our team's playing like a bunch of old ladies and it's all enough to sour the milk in your tea. Do you know Dickie Lockwood?

Harry	Not personally, I'm told he's signed for Heckmondwike for a king's ransom, I know that.
Herbert	The only *amateur* rugby player to stroll round in leather soled shoes and go for his dinner at Bradford Midland Hotel. I saw him play for England agin the Scots. Played like three backs rolled into one. Wonderful. If I'd known Hecky were on the prowl I'd o' sent a welcoming party and kidnapped him. Do you think he'd blow them out and sign for us?
Harry	Him moving club again so quick, might be somewhat imprudent?
Herbert	Suspicious. Aye. Last thing we need's Reverend Frank *'bell book and candle'* Marshall himself excommunicating us, his own club, from the Rugby Union. We need something though. Keep losing like this and crowds'll drop off.
Harry	Gate receipts plummet.
Herbert	Not good. We need a proper up and at 'em forward.
Harry	Stop us getting bullied in the middle.
Herbert	A big piledriving powerhouse, whatever the cost.
Harry	Something to light our fire, rekindle the passions...

Herbert	Something different?
Harry	Exotic.
Herbert	Foreign?
Harry	Worse. Welsh. There is one name I've heard mentioned… they reckon he's the finest thing to come out of the valleys…
Herbert	Since the steam powered locomotive to England!? I like him already!

Both stop their conversation. Enter Reverend Marshall.

Rev	You like who already?
Herbert	(*shocked*) Reverend Marshall.
Rev	Mr Dalton, Harry (*pause*) am I interrupting some important conversation? You like who already?
Bessie	Oh they were just discussing the vagaries of trade and commerce.
Rev	Were they indeed. How very dull.
Bessie	I quite agree Reverend Dalton.
Harry	Marshall.
Bessie	Marshall Dalton.
Harry	Reverend Marshall!

Bessie	Reverend Marshall! Got there in the end! (*pause*) So what do you do for a living then Reverend Marshall?

All pause, and look at Bessie, who realizes her mistake with a shriek of embarrassed laughter.

Bessie	Oh I declare! Sorry, still a bit early in the day for me!
Herbert	Miss Butterworth is in the music hall Reverend. Doubtless you're familiar…?
Rev	You know perfectly well I am not. What's more I lend my fulsome support and prayers to Mrs Ormiston Chant of the Purity Party in her fervent desire to see these dens of vice closed down entirely.

Awkward pause. Harry speaks before Bessie does.

Harry	Let's look forward to the game shall we, and *pray* it cheers our hearts eh Reverend?
Rev	Let us first and foremost pray it is played in the right spirit.
Herbert	And we win whatever the cost.

The sound of a crowd comes in, boos etc. The band plays as Herbert, Harry and the Reverend look on as West Broughton lose. Bessie is bored rigid.

Rev	Fine play the Brighouse team, excellent try.

Herbert   What?! Come on Wests! Stand up to 'em!
           Fight! Where's your backbone eh?

More crowd noise and booing. Finally the final whistle
goes.

Rev   Shake hands and applaud the victors from
           the field West Broughton. People booing,
           after such a sterling effort from both teams.
           Appalling. Simply appalling. Give thanks
           gentlemen… a good game was played… it
           matters not who won.

Herbert   It does to the supporters, and by jingo
           Reverend it more than does to me. I hate
           losing. Hence I never do it for long.

Rev   This just underlines the importance of proper
           schooling.

Herbert   I beg your pardon?

Rev   There are times Herbert, when I wonder if
           you understand the game at all. My dear
           man it belongs more in the realm of religious
           life than that of *trade*. The merchant classes
           may be able to buy the clubs… but they can
           never *own* the game. A very good day to you
           all.

The Reverend exits. Herbert is spitting blood.

Herbert   The confounded cheek! I don't understand
           the game?! *"Than that of trade!!"* We'll see
           about that! Harry… that Welshman… you

see to it he gets aboard said locomotive,
immediately!

SCENE 3
A Welsh hymn comes in. Lights focus on one man, in the
dark, light just on the blackened face of **Lewy Jenkins**. It's
as if he's in a cage, tired, he has been bent over all day
hewing coal, but he is a tall, athletic young man. Someone
hands him a bucket and he takes his dirty vest off and
washes himself down. Someone throws him a rugby ball,
and a game commences. The singing continues, gentle
underscoring, as his Mother speaks.

Ma   Run Lewy, my darling boy! Don't let them
                catch you! I knew when you was inside me
                you was strong... kick like a mule didn't
                you? Your Da said back row forward the
                second he saw you.

This speech below is spread among the entire cast as if they
are locals watching him. Harry Stockwell joins them.

                Go Jenkins boy, go! Flail them!
                Show no mercy, like a lion of the valleys he
                is!! Magnificent! What an athlete!
                One of our very own, making us so proud he
                is... He'll play for Wales... oh imagine it...
                knocking merry hell out of those English!

                Money can't buy that boy! That is real riches.
                A proper hero he'll be... like... Spartacus...
                like... Robin Hood... Like Owen
                Glendower...
                We love that boy like he was our own.

18

Ma   Your old da'd be proud if he was still here
            son... but he barely even held you... not six
            months after you came in he went out, good
            as passed each other didn't you? Coal
            dust... on his chest, up his nose, in his eyes,
            in his ears... most of all... in his heart I
            reckon. Just weighed down with it. Some
            was born to ride in carriages see... and some
            to scrat around on their bellies way
            underground... he just didn't get lucky that's
            all... and neither have you.

Lewy emerges from the cage to be surrounded by (*Welsh*)
kids all shouting Lewy! Lewy! Waving cigarette cards at
him and wanting him to sign it for them, he happily signs
them. last in line is a smiling Harry Stockwell.

Kid   Lewy Jenkins signed my card...

            He even touched me on my forehead!

2nd   He stepped on my big toe!

3rd   (*overjoyed*) He knocked my dad's gnasher's
            out in a scrum last week! Look I kept 'em as
            a souvenir!

The kid pulls out his old man's gnashers to show everyone.

Harry   Hello Lewy.

Lewy looks blankly at Harry, as he puts on a clean shirt, a
collar, a jacket, slowly he is transformed. Before him now is
Harry Stockwell.

Harry	You're making hell of a name for yourself.
Lewy	Who are you?
Harry	Harry Stockwell, and I've got a proposition to put to you.

Harry takes a folded piece of paper from his inside pocket. The choral singing comes back in as Lewy and Harry move downstage and take seats. It fades out, Lewy is deep in thought. He hands the paper back to Harry.

Lewy	I dunno to be honest. To tell you the truth Mr Stockwell… it feels… dirty.
Harry	Dirty as digging coal? Don't tell me you were born to be a miner. Old afore you time, back bent, chest all silted up.
Lewy	Nobody's born for that. It's hard work, but you get used to it.
Harry	I've heard fellers say the same about champagne and caviar… I know which I'd prefer.
Lewy	My old teacher, Mr Griffiths, taught us that to play was everything. "*A gift from God*", he said, to be young and fit enough… worth more than any amount of money.
Harry	He was right. To play is everything… but to play and make *money*… well that's twice times everything with bells on.

Harry departs, with the paper. Lewy is alone, he thinks. In comes the choir, a mournful Welsh choral piece. His old teacher comes to him.

Teacher   It's just not very much for a man's soul that's all. All those boys in school now… all they ask me about is you… what'll they say?

Harry   They'll say he bettered himself like he was entitled to do.

Teacher   They will. But they won't say he was our hero in the face of defeat… they won't sing songs of his dashing flair, his pace and power, or talk all night of his finest hour.

Harry   Make your mind up. It's a lot of money Lewy, where will a lad like you ever see that eh?

Now his dear old Ma appears.

Ma   Going where!?

Lewy   Yorkshire Ma, it's not exactly the moon!

Ma   Leaving your poor old Ma as she gets older are you? How could you!? Oh shame on you, turncoat you nothing else, my own son! My own flesh and blood You've broken my heart you…

Lewy   There's fifty pounds here.

Ma   Oh, is there?

21

Lewy	And I'll send more.
Ma	No finer boy ever walked these hills! I'll kill any man says a word against him! Go go go to Yorkshire my lad, they're smashing people up there, just like us I've heard, coalminers, drinkers, brawlers and swearers, tarts and philanderers, oh you'll be at home up there alright!
Lewy	So long Ma.
Ma	(*soft*) So long my Lewy. I always knew you'd make it. Knees and elbows son! Run straight. Don't let them catch you.

The sound of a train comes in. Lewy settles down to enjoy the ride.

SCENE 4
Herbert greets Lewy – takes him straight to the changing room.

Lewy	Mr Dalton?
Herbert	Welcome to West Broughton! Not much of a place, but well, it's mine. I hear you're the finest thing since automated weaving gear!
Lewy	That's me, faster than a speeding shuttle!
Herbert	You'll be right happy here, the epi centre of industrial and sporting prowess! When my old feller started his first mill here there was

nothing but green fields… now the only bit
of grass for a mile or more is us rugby field!
Oh we've come a long way in a short time
lad! Come and meet your new team mates,
match kicks off in half an hour, straight in at
deep end eh?

Herbert & Lewy enter the West Broughton changing room.

Herbert   Boys, be up standing to meet your new
           mucker! Lewy Jenkins.

All stand up to greet Lewy.

Lewy   Alright fellas.

George   Lewy Jenkins? I've heard all about you mate!

Herbert   This is George, our top try scorer for the past
           three seasons.

Lewy   George Wilkinson?

George   (*elated*) That's me! Do you hear that Gil!
           They've heard of me in Wales!!

Gil   Aye, it's *what* they've heard worries me.

George   And this is Gil Gannon. He's so tight he buys
           2nd hand sandwiches!

Gil   George does the jokes round here so hang
           onto your return ticket.

George   The famous miserable swine of old West

Broughton! A night out with him makes you think a dose of diptheria might not be all that bad. Have a peg Lewy. In fact here, have mine.

Lewy   I have never seen a man give up his peg in a dressing room yet. That's very generous George.

George   I just like to make a fellow feel welcome, bit of right respect, do unto others…

Lewy   Put it there, you'll do for me man.

They shake hands. Then Lewy holds his hand out to Gil, who doesn't respond.

Gil   Long way from home aren't you?

Lewy   Oh I dunno, I reckon one rain sodden dump full of tight fisted buggers not washed since the midwife done it, is heck of a lot like another really.

George   I reckon so.

Lewy   I think I'm gonna like it here.

George does a big wink at Lewy as Gil picks up his rugby drawers. There is a huge hole in the backside of them.

Gil   Alright which maestro of mirth's done this!?

Lewy   Done what?

Gil	Cut the backside out of me drawers!?
Lewy	Don't look at me, I only just got here!
Gil	George?
George	(*sweetness*) Yes Gilbert old bean, did you call?
Gil	Don't come the choirboy wi' me! "Yes Gilbert?" my backside!
Lewy	On public view, Might I recommend buying some moth balls?
Herbert	Hell of a bloody moth!
George	It might make you more popular with the ladies Gil have you thought of that?
Lewy	See? Every cloud and all that. Who knows it might catch on?
George	More likely with southern teams than up here.
Gil	Come on own up, who's done it!?
Herbert	I've heard of showing the other team a clean pair of heels but a clean pair of cheeks, now that's new.
Lewy	They are clean aren't they Gil?
Gil	None of your bloody business!

George	If it keeps you moving out there Gil then no bad thing.
Gil	What am I gonna do now? I can't go out and play wi' me backside hung out!
Herbert	Course you can, team first, personal comfort second.
Lewy	Promise not to fart in any rucks, and I don't mind.
George	Me neither.
Gil	Ha bloody ha! Believe it or not I bloody do! Flamin hell's fire!
Herbert	Alright boys, settle down, let's get set for a big game today, some proper blood bustin, rawboned power and fury out there today! I know you all want to win, make the club proud, the supporters happy, am I right?
All	Aye aye Mr Dalton.
Herbert	I said am I right?
All	Yeh!!
Herbert	Good lads. Now get out there and get stuck in, and Gil, don't go making an arse of yourself!

All laugh, except Gil.

| Gil | Mr Dalton, may I have a word. |

They move to a private corner.

| Gil | How much are you paying the blow in? |

| Herbert | I beg your pardon? |

| Gil | Lewy come lately, what's he on, more than't rest of us? |

| Herbert | Gilbert really… such a suspicious mind! May I remind you that the curse of Trade Unionism does not extend to this dressing room! I couldn't possibly discuss any private arrangement I may have come to with Mr Jenkins, and I'm not saying I have, with another player. Who knows if you stick as tight to him on the field as you do that flaming union handbook we might even win for a change! |

He addresses the whole dressing room now.

> Have a good game boys, I want to see plenty of pride and passion! And get Gil some new knickers for God's sake!

SCENE 5
Rugby Sequence. The referee appears in bowler hat, cigar in mouth.

| Referee | Afternoon gentlemen, all set for a good, fair, rousing but sportsmanlike encounter eh? |

27

Gil turns to his fellow players.

Gil   Aye. Right lads, I want to see blood and guts
               in the mud! Let's kill em!!

The game begins. A thunderous heaving of grunts and
shouts as the ball is fought and grappled for. Lewy is right
to the fore. The crowd roars and the score board reads West
Broughton. This sequence halts – stops dead and the
ensemble morph into spectators in the directors box.

Rev   Herbert… there would appear to be a
               newcomer in our ranks.

Herbert   Yes Reverend there does. And you can see
               what a difference he makes right off. Now
               settle down and watch the team that'll win
               the Yorkshire Cup. And I'll tell you why,
               pride. Pride in the shirt, the town. The same
               people who work for me come out, rain or
               shine, to support the team, *their* team! They
               work hard all week, we give them something
               to cheer of a Saturday, be proud of. Can't put
               a price on that.

Rev   How very moving. What price has the
               newcomer placed upon his services?

All stop their cheering and turn sharply to look at Herbert.

Herbert   Reverend, this is hardly the moment.

Rev   Whyever not? Is it embarrassing for you?

Herbert	No.
Rev	It ought to be.
Herbert	It isn't.
Rev	I recall a time when this game was a decent pastime, for respectable individuals.
Herbert	Each with his own little silver spoon.
Rev	And a clear conscience.
Herbert	Lewy asked if he could play for us, and we obliged him.
Rev	Do you expect me to believe that?
Herbert	Yes.
Rev	Look at it, drunken crowds, appalling behaviour on the pitch and in the stands. Umpires *assaulted* by spectators… whoever heard of it? And why? Because the core values have been slowly destroyed… by greed. Avarice! It will end up just like Association football, run by people who cannot even spell their own name.
Harry	Might not be able to spell… but they can all count.

There is a cold and icy stand off between the Reverend and Herbert.

Rev   Good day to you. Rest assured… this shall
             not be allowed to pass.

Exit Reverend Marshall. None speaks for a few seconds.
Then Harry breaks it.

Harry   I can't say for certain… But I don't think he's
             very happy.

Herbert   Who cares we're winning! Come on lads
             keep it up!

The sound of the crowd roaring as the scoreboard ticks over
and West Broughton have won. Music comes in to take us
through to the end of the match. Herbert is delighted, but
concerned also.

SCENE 6

The Bridge Hotel. Bessie enters begins silent, preparations
for a music hall number, learning the words and working
out a dance step. Gil Gannon occupies a table with George,
who is rather more interested in Bessie, who looks for
somewhere to put the words of the song she is learning.

Gil   Special gents changing rooms, we travel 3rd
             class to away matches, they go first. They get
             proper hotels we get glorified dosshouses,
             they get wine we get beer.

George   Aye well that's life innit? Them and us,
             always has been, always will be.

Gil   Always will be while we go on accepting it.

Bessie	(*to George*) Would you mind holding something for me sweetheart?
George	No, not at all.
Gil	3rd class citizens here, on the train, on the pitch…
George	Do you know 'The Ratcatcher's Daughter'?
Gil	Are you listening?
Bessie	Not personally no.
George	I mean the song.

He sings a brief snatch, suddenly he stops dead. Enter Annie. George attempts to hide behind the sheet of music, fails.

Annie	Did I not say straight home after the game? What are you doing if you don't mind my asking?
Bessie	He's holding my music.
Annie	Well let her hold her own music.
George	Annie, I've had one pint with Gil here, and I promise you, I haven't enjoyed it, honest!
Annie	You been talking politics again Gil?
Gil	How do you know?

Annie	The place is empty, like a flaming morgue in here. Why do you have to come in here anyway? The Bridge Hotel, what if there's overlookers and mill managers in? It's not proper.
Gil	Aye, they are a bit beneath us Annie.
George	She didn't mean that. Gil you're my best mate, since so high?
Gil	I reckon.
George	And old mates can be like straight with each other, right?
Gil	I reckon.
George	Right. You are one long faced pain in the gizzard! I'm just levelling with you.
Gil	And what if I levelled you for saying that?
George	Here I am old pal you have a try!
Annie	Alright alright that's enough!

Lewy enters as Bessie speaks.

Bessie	May I remind you this is a proper high class establishment catering for proper respectable citizens and the first one to ask what I'm doing here is out!
Annie	(*pause*) What you doing here then?

George	Don't worry we're going. Before 2nd hand sandwiches here gives us heart failure wi' laughing! Union clap trap, I'm sick of it. Look, we played, we won, I got me little bonus in me boots, I have a good bed, a comfy chair and a bacon joint at home, I'm married to Annie, we're having a little un, it in't raining, much... what else?
Annie	(*thinks*) The midden got emptied yesterday so...
George	Life's bloody great!
Gil	Wait till he cuts your wages! What then? It'll be where's union? what's union doing!?
Bessie	Gil, why don't you try a bit of charm instead... when you want a gent to buy you a drink and throw his cash about, you don't say, "bit of a pot belly if you don't mind me saying, ooh getting a bit thin on top aren't we? I bet you don't exactly send your missis into screaming fits neither..." Because it won't work, but if you...

Goes into flirt mode, gushes etc, now she sees and addresses Lewy.

	Oh my... well... we are a handsome dashing devil aren't we now?
Gil	Bessie, I want them to listen to important political discourse.

Annie	Not buy him beef and dumplings, a jug full of gin, then stick their tongue in his ear.
Bessie	Suit yourself, no odds to me flower. I tried.
George	Lewy Jenkins... our new best mucker! This here's our Annie.
Bessie	Hello Lewy. Bessie Butterworth.
Lewy	Miss Butterworth. Mrs Wilkinson.
Annie	Manners!
Bessie	He can't be local.
Lewy	May I get anyone a drink? Gil? George?
George	Aye I'll have…
Annie	No he won't, thank you very much. We are leaving.
Gil	And I have a meeting to attend, in Bradford... political business.
Bessie	And there'll be plenty high jinks there I warrant you! Golly what laughs!
Annie	Miss Butterworth might join you, she's partial to the odd jug of gin I understand.
Bessie	Well you understand wrong dearie cos I never touch the stuff. And I make my own dumplings. You can bring the beef, Mr Jenkins.

Annie	(*appalled*) Tart.

George nearly chokes on his beer.

Lewy	(*pause*) Trade Unions Gil, the working man's best friend, I quite agree.
Gil	Glad you think so.
Lewy	I've come to see Harry.
Annie	George?
Bessie	He's out, on business.
Lewy	Good for Harry.
Gil	It always seems to be.
Annie	George!
Lewy	I can wait. I'll have a pint of Stockwell's Ale, if I may.
Bessie	I might be a few things pet lamb, but a barmaid's not one of 'em.
Annie	Wouldn't be so bad if it was.
George	Annie!
Lewy	Well if you can't serve me a pint, you'd better sing for me… to pass the time.
Bessie	Show don't start till eight pumpkin, and it's ninepence on the door.

Lewy	Oh I'll be back later, with my ninepence, don't worry about that. Sing (*names a Welsh hymn*)
Bessie	I'd love to sweetheart… but I've never heard of it.
Lewy	Really? You never sang it in church when you was little?
Annie	Oh, as if!
Bessie	Not in Welsh. Why don't you sing it for me.

So he does. Bessie is very taken with him. Harry enters, unseen by them initially, instantly suspicious of Lewy & Bessie together, waits for Lewy to finish the song. He applauds, only now do they see him.

Harry	Lewy, you are one heck of a talented feller!
Bessie	Just what I was thinking.
George	Lewy Jenkins! Rugby footballer… singer… romantic hero. Well played today Lewy… we're all glad you're here. Annie, lead the way.
Lewy	You're welcome. Night George, Annie.

Exit Annie & George. Lewy peers round the room at them, maybe Gil and Harry aren't quite so glad as George is?

Harry	Well… you are surely making a heck of a big impression Lewy!

Bessie	He is.
Harry	As you've doubtless gathered, Bessie is the beauty of this operation, whilst I am the brains.
Bessie	Don't believe a word he says.
Gil	Seriously, don't.
Lewy	I reckon she's the beauty and the brains.
Gil	What's that make you then Harry?
Harry	(*terse*) The boss. You not got anywhere to be Gil?
Lewy	I just came by, so you can show me the Red Lion actually.
Harry	I'll get the keys of it.
Bessie	Oh Lewy, don't take that *dreadful* Red Lion place... I want you to come in here!
Lewy	Well I'm sure it's not that far away.
Bessie	Oh I could never visit there... it's hardly the right sort of place for a *lady*.
Harry	No, it's not. Like he says, drop by when you want.
Gil	Won't this make him competition for you?

Harry	Nothing wrong with a bit of competition.
Lewy	No no no... makes the world go round.
Bessie	What if his beer's better than yours?
Harry	What if.
Gil	And his entertainment's of a higher calibre?
Harry	Wouldn't be hard.
Bessie	And he's just not as all round objectionable?
Lewy	Oh I think the entertainment here is the finest for a long way Harry.
Bessie	Thank you.
Gil	Well... don't take offence, but I have to go.
Harry	I never could Gil, have a nice evening.
Gil	A meeting of the newly formed Independent Labour Party, Lewy, over in Bradford... representing the workers... you're welcome to join us.
Lewy	I'd... well I would but...
Harry	He's a businessman now Gil... swapped sides... in't that right Lewy?

No reply from Lewy, who feels awkward. Gil eyes him coldly.

Gil	Word of advice Lewy. Don't get too thick with any of 'em.

Exit Gil. Harry eyes Bessie and Lewy, coldly. Tension, finally Bessie breaks it.

Bessie	What's it say about this town when we have to go all the way to Wales to fetch a real man, eh Harry?
Harry	(*pause/terse*) No idea. Well much as I could revel in this jolly banter all night, the Red Lion... it's one of our hostelries in need of a little love and attention. It has a great deal of... hitherto unrealized potential. Hence my delight at securing a tenant of your... *stature* and renown. Actually it was my dear uncle Joshua's pub... yes... he passed away right behind the bar.
Lewy	Really? What of?
Harry	Strangulation.
Lewy	Oh dear, how very sad.
Bessie	Not to them that knew him.
Harry	Yes, very sad... he and his third wife, Aggie, had a particularly popular party trick, they made a lot of money out of.
Bessie	Must you?
Harry	Aye. They could both pee in a pint pot at the same time.

Bessie	Harry!
Lewy	(*pause*) I'm absolutely fascinated by that, and desperate to know how they did it, aren't you Bessie?
Bessie	No.
Harry	Well she used to squat down over it, stark naked…
Bessie	Do you have to?
Harry	Then he'd stand in front of her, and she'd bob her head down like this, you see, then he'd pee down the back of her neck, it'd run down her backbone, down the crack of her arse… aye… till it met with her stream and both would then flow perfectly into aforesaid vessel. (*pause*) Now that is what I call entertainment!
Lewy	The old turns were the best eh.
Harry	Oh yes, far and away. Just think Lewy… a piece of property, all of your very own. This'll be the first time you've had that won't it? Since you were down the mines. I always say a feller is wise to look after his own property… and keep his hands off other people's.
Lewy	I'm not sure I follow your drift Harry?
Harry	Merely observing. Feller can land himself in

a lot of trouble, putting his grubby mits on that which he does *not* own. More than he can handle.

Neither man speaks for an awkward moment. Harry holds the keys of the pub up, hands them to Lewy. Bessie glares at him, contemptuously.

Harry   (*to Bessie*) Why don't you go ready yourself
                 for the show? I don't pay you to stand
                 around yapping. (*to Lewy*) Well there's the
                 keys. All yours now. Best of luck.

Bessie looks at Harry with contempt. Lewy is tempted to hit him.

SCENE 7
Reverend Marshall takes his place in the pulpit.

Rev   We bring ourselves closer to God not only
                 through the gospel and it's teaching, but
                 through sporting prowess also... the Lord has
                 bestowed upon us physical gifts that he
                 intends us to use for His purposes. The game
                 of rugby football embodies Christianity in
                 it's most muscular form. For it is through a
                 healthy body that we achieve a healthy
                 mind, and thus a cleansed and powerful
                 spirit. Muscular Christianity. Nothing could
                 prepare our young men better for the
                 challenges of life that await both here at
                 home and far away in the darkest corners of
                 the earth. But there are temptations to be
                 overcome. In the brave days of old, in the

public games of the Spartans and the
Athenians, the victor was crowned with a
wreath, not of gold, but of the leaves of the
wild olive. But in these degenerate days,
after 1800 years of the high moral teaching
and influence of Christianity, some would
say our young sportsmen are to be bribed to
victory by the secret application of 'palm oil'
and to have their morals corrupted and their
minds debased.

Now the Reverend gets more passionate.

Rev M   It is time to stand up against this malign
               influence! To confront those who know the
               price of everything and the value of nothing!
               To protect our young menfolk from the evils
               of professionalism, and to remove sport once
               and for all from the dictats of *business*, of
               greed... what profit a man if he gain the
               whole world and loses his immortal soul?
               We must be steadfast, show no mercy,
               nothing but iron rigour. It is our sworn duty
               to our young. So, now we pray that they
               make us proud and that we do not fail them
               in return.

Lewy looks around uncomfortably. Herbert is furious. The
Reverend fixes him with a stare as a hymn comes in. The
service ends. The reverend comes off the pulpit and exits
the church.

Lewy   For a man of God... he doesn't have a very
               generous nature does he?

Herbert	Nor the foggiest idea how this modern world works either. Come on, let's get some fresh air. (*They walk*) I'm gonna make you team captain, in charge. A leader of men. It changes the way you think... look at things
Lewy	I'm honoured Mr Dalton... but Gil won't like that will he?
Herbert	Gil just works at my mill and plays for the team, he doesn't run either, in spite of what he might think. I want to win the Yorkshire Cup... biggest competition in the land. There's more millionaires in Yorkshire than anywhere else in the world and do you know why that is?
Lewy	You're all tight as a fish's arse in a sand storm.
Herbert	Exactly... eh? Well... aye there's that... but it's also because we mix hard graft with sharp nouse. Aye. Do fish get in sand storms? Never mind. You've come to the very centre of the game... here and in Lancashire as well, And it sickens them RFU lot. Old stuffed shirts, like the Reverend, trying to hold back the tide... take rugby back to being a gents only public school la de dah game. They won't. These are different times... new ideas, new inventions, electricity, amazing... I was taught in bible class only the Almighty himself could say let there be light... now we can all say it at the turn of a switch! What's that tell you?

Lewy	The Almighty needs a few new tricks?
Herbert	Oh and he'll find 'em don't worry. There's a feller in New York built a machine you can talk into at one end... down a wire... and a feller 5 mile away on the other end can hear *every* word you say. Unbelievable! Think what you could do with that!
Lewy	Fall out in lumps with people 5 mile away as well as here!
Herbert	Do business with them! In the blink of an eye! What else can they do? These engineers, inventors? Who knows. It's like my weaving machines... people said they'd put folk out of work and they'd starve... they didn't... they put more in work, on better pay. Progress... that's what Gilbert needs to understand... them and their radical ideas, guaranteed fixed wages, regardless of the market! Have you ever heard the like of it!? They're even more dangerous than the reverend... and they'd both destroy everything we're seeking to achieve. Progress!
Lewy	I come from a long line of coalminers Mr Dalton... I agree with Trade unions.
Herbert	Lewy, that's where you've come from... but it's not where you're going to. The future's bright... we're gonna win that Yorkshire Cup... be the best team in the land.

As Lewy speaks the Reverend enters the space, as if coming down from the pulpit, or exiting the church.

Lewy   You've been good with me Mr Dalton, put me in a place I never thought I'd get to. I won't let you down. I just want to play, and win, and be treated fair. I like this town, these people, good hardworking rugby folk, just like home. I've got big plans too Mr Dalton. I've got some innovations to make in our playing style, I want us to play with 4 three quarters, two on each side… it gives more width and pace.

Herbert   This is what I'm paying you for!

Now Lewy sees the Reverend. He nods coldly at him as he exits. Now the Reverend and Herbert eyeball one another.

Herbert   I've just made him captain of the team. We need leadership. We need to run a more…

Rev   *Professional* operation?

Herbert   Organized.

Rev   I cannot disagree more powerfully. I intend to put a proposal to the next board meeting, that in view of the murky financial situation regarding the employment of this man Jenkins, we dispense with his services, before he grows too accustomed to our hospitality.

Herbert   Do you think anyone'll agree with you? Dispense with the best player we've got.

Rev	In a few weeks from now we will be attending the 1893 AGM of the Rugby Football Union.
Herbert	And?
Rev	This selfless act would set an example.
Herbert	Of?
Rev	The spirit of noble amateurism that is the very core of our game.
Herbert	Is it? The Rugby Union aren't even sure themselves what to do about this. The proposal regarding payments for broken time at work might well be accepted.
Rev	This is precisely why we have to stand, and now. This broken time charade must be stamped out immediately.
Herbert	Let's face it half the clubs in the country are greasing the players palms are they not?
Rev	Half the miners and weavers in the country drink themselves to oblivion on Saturday and then retire homeward to beat their wives. Is that a reason for everyone to do so? Make no mistake this is a battle for the soul of our sport. Sending Mr Jenkins on his way would set an excellent precedent in the fight against professionalism.
Herbert	No-one is advocating professionalism. Broken time means recompensing the

working lads for the wages lost, and for travelling to and from games, I for one believe it to be a fair one.

Rev
Even if that is what we are doing, which I now powerfully suspect it is not, it is professionalism by the back door and it will open the floodgates.

Herbert
I can't agree, the broken time proposal is the best defence against professionalism!

Rev
Payment is payment, it matters not what guise you clothe it in. Sport is about the finest pitting their skills against the finest, for love of the game, the glory of God and country. It springs from the purest and noblest instincts. It should not be perverted to fill the pockets of young upstarts, so they might strut about celebrating nothing but their own vanity.

Herbert
Some of them do get a bit above themselves it has to be said.

Rev
As they will when they are misdirected. They are young and ill educated. It is our duty to protect all the working folk from themselves, not just at work, but also at leisure.

Herbert
Yes, and perhaps place a time limit on laughter, or the width of a smile to boot.

Rev
Facetious comment is both vulgar and juvenile. Look what is happening with

Association football, and now it is the turn of Rugby! One day the working classes with their Independent Labour Party will take control entirely and what then? Chaos, revolution, civilization destroyed utterly!

Herbert Look for the life in me I cannot see how covering them for broken time at work is somehow poisoning their immortal souls or destroying civilization as we know it! Neither do I see how we *'protect'* them from themselves by denying them the right to play the game they love because they cannot afford to! Which is what the RFU and the rest of them flaming jackals in London are trying to achieve by the way! Enforce the amateur principle and the working lads won't be able to play anymore, then where would we be?

Rev It matters not. The principle is all that counts. Herbert you are too mired in the world of commerce. Sport is about something much more valuable than money!

Herbert In my experience people who say things like that have never set foot in a poorhouse. All my life I've paid a man for what he did, and I've expected to be paid for what I do for him.

Rev I warn you… reduce rugby to the level of a simple transaction between mere businessmen… and we will all be the loser.

Herbert All this at the same time as this club pays the expenses of it's gentlemen players without a second thought.

Rev   It is unreasonable to expect decent people to cover the cost of their own travel, that is all the payment is for, this is entirely different and you know it.

Herbert   No I don't. We charge at the gate don't we? Isn't that a simple transaction? Who is it they come to see? Lewy, Gil Gannon, George Wilkinson. The working players have improved the game no end since it was a pastime for gentlemen alone.

Rev   That in itself is arguable. There is a level of brute thuggery on the field now that was unheard of 20 years ago. They either play the game for the love of it, or not at all. I move we thank Mr Jenkins for his efforts on Saturday and bid him farewell.

Herbert   It would destroy this club!

Rev   It will save the game!

Both men are furious. There is a pause, a poisoned atmosphere.

Rev   Tell me, there is a recession looming in the textile industry is there not?

Herbert   Not looming no, it's here. Already bringing chaos and destruction in other towns... difficult times alright.

Rev	And it may be the death of your business, might it not?
Herbert	(*coldly*) Not if I can help it. Your point?
Rev	When you... false gods... of trade have succumbed to the dust from whence you came... what will be left?
Herbert	Hunger.
Rev	Man... Mr Dalton... cannot live on bread alone.
Herbert	No. He needs the odd roll of bacon now and then as well.
Rev	The amateur principle is the very soul of the game. There can be no compromise.
Herbert	Lose my business... Reverend Frank Marshall... and my team? Know this man... not likely. Not bloody likely!

Herbert storms off, furious, leaving the Reverend.

SCENE 8
A sign reads: **Yorkshire Cup 1st round West Broughton versus Wakefield Trinity**. The team forms around Lewy.

Lewy	Alright lads, this is just the start, our first Yorkshire Cup of many. You can be part of something historic, something folks will talk about, that others will have to live up to,

long after we're gone. We're the lucky ones, that have this chance, we happy few, we band of brothers, aye those that are safely up in the stands will look down on us this day and say...

Gil   Are they right in their heads?

Lewy   And the answer will be...

All   NO!!!

Lewy   Let's go!

The ball comes out and the game begins. Enter the referee in bowler hat with cigar as usual. This is a lengthy rugby sequence, plenty grunting, gasping, heaving, punches thrown, the crowd roars.

Sign - Yorkshire Cup 2nd round West Broughton versus Leeds.

From there it moves **to Yorkshire Cup Quarter Final West Broughton versus Hull**.

George takes a pass, he runs (*on the spot*) the length of the field to score a try. Annie leaps in the air, screaming, then comes down and holds her belly. She is about to have the baby.

Annie is surrounded by people as the heaving mass of the rugby scrum becomes the birth pangs of a woman in labour, this ends with the noise of a baby crying and George emerges from the scrum with the ball having morphed into a baby. He gazes at it in wonder. Annie's cries subside.

Annie	George…
George	Look... it's... it's...
Annie	I know what it is! Did we win?
George	Oh yes... we won... we're in the semi final!
Annie	Thank God.
George	We've got a son Annie! Oh what a… what a… what a son!
Annie	Aye. And what a time to be born.
George	Midway through a Yorkshire cup quarter final!
Gil	That's got to be a sign!
Lewy	This child is blessed!
Gil	What shall we call him?
George	(*thinks*) Semi final!
Lewy	Can't call him that! What if we're in the final come the christening?
Gil	He's right. *Final* Wilkinson it is.
George	Aye, that's a proper Yorkshire name, isn't it lad?
Annie	Er… we'll call him Arthur thanks very much.

Gil   Final Arthur?

Annie   Arthur *Wilkinson*! After my grandfather and
           George's dad. Let's just hope he doesn't take
           after either, God rest 'em.

George   Arthur… I'm passing you back to your mum,
           do as she says. God knows I have to.

He gives her the baby back, but still can't take his eyes off
it.

Lewy   I brought us some bottles round, hope you
           don't mind Annie?

Lewy hands the bottles out. There's a knock on the door.
Bessie enters.

George   Bessie!

Bessie   I won't stop… I've just come to congratulate
           you.

George   Thank you love, it were hard game but we
           deserved it.

Gil/ Lewy Definitely.

Bessie   On the baby!

George   Oh aye, yeah… blow me down… I still can't
           believe it… a baby!

Lewy   I'm glad you've come. I er… I've been…

George	He's been hoping you blow that snake in the grass Harry out, no one likes him, come and work for Lewy, he... (*points dramatically at Lewy*) him there... is a cracking fellow!

Lewy looks at her for an answer. She looks away as George continues.

George	There you see... you know I'm right. Gil did you see me leave 'em all for dead out there today?
Gil	I did. And I saw Lewy carry five blokes 15 yards over the line with him as well.
George	To Lewy Jenkins, the Welsh... (*thinks*) wizard!
All	To Lewy Jenkins the Welsh wizard!
Lewy	To my dear old Yorkshire comrades! Who've made me feel so at home.
Bessie	Mercy me, all brothers together in here aren't we?
George	We're a team Bessie... all brothers... that's right... I love you Gil Gannon! And you Lewy Jenkins!
Bessie	What about Annie?
George	Aye come on love don't be laid in bed all day we've got guests.

Bessie	I didn't mean that!
George	But I'm not just a brother... I'm a dad! His little fist round my finger... so beautiful... so little... his little fist...
Annie	Get a grip George! Crying like a babby yourself man.
George	I can't help it. I can't... My Annie... my... my Annie!

George curls up beside Annie and falls asleep. Image/sense of Annie as having two babies not one.

Gil	He'll never alter.
Bessie	Leave him be Gil. He's happy that's all.
Gil	There's no harm in him. Night night.

Exit Gil.

Bessie	I envy them.
Lewy	Then don't go back to him, George is right, he's a toad.
Bessie	Harry's done a lot for me in the past.
Lewy	The past... that's where you've come from... but it's not where you're going to.

He takes hold of her and kisses her.

These days are different Bessie… people like us can earn money… real money… and have our freedom… I want to take it in both hands… and to hell with Harry, Reverend Marshall and all of them old farts at the RFU with him.

SCENE 9

The Rugby Football Union AGM 1893. The atmosphere is volatile. A real sense of Reverend Marshall working the room here, moving among the delegates, pressing the flesh etc.

Chair   Order Gentlemen please!! I would like to convene this 1893 Annual General Meeting of the Rugby Football Union. The Yorkshire Rugby Union propose the following: firstly that we limit the migration of players or transfer of services, secondly to grant reasonable concessions by allowing the men to be paid for loss of wages due to broken time… And lastly far greater penalties to be imposed for professionalism!

There is uproar and discord at this. Some cheer, others boo.

1st   What rights or control do clubs have over a player who is officially an amateur but in reality is taking home a small fortune for which there exists no written contract of employment?

2nd   This supposed sham amateurism is the worst of all worlds! At least professionalism runs along properly organized lines the same as any other business! At present we have no idea what expenditure is being incurred on players because it is all done cloak and dagger.

3rd   If we are to have professionalism let us have it and be honest about it. But don't let us go for bastard subterfuges!

4th   Professionalism will lead to the bankruptcy of the clubs! There isn't the money in rugby to support it, simple as that!

Much uproar at that. It's getting very heated.

Herbert   Surely the broken time compromise, of recompensing working players for the wages they lose through playing and travelling is the fairest way forward!?

Rev M   Gentlemen why is it that this entire debate revolves around the working players only? What right have they to claim this game as their own? They have poisoned it, as much with their brute thuggery on the field as with their tawdry obsession with money away from it!

5th   Under the guise of broken time the Yorkshire and Lancashire clubs with their *grubbily* acquired wealth will be free to pay the players whatever they want, which will lead to greater migration! Don't be fooled!

Rev M   Any player even suspected of
             professionalism should have to prove his
             innocence and not the other way around as
             in any court of law. Gentlemen I say no
             mercy but iron rigour! Guilty until proven
             innocent!

Tensions boil over, private rows flare up.

Chair   Order! Gentlemen order!! Those in favour of
             the Broken Time Payments 136... those
             against... 282!

Pandemonium, cheering from some, bitter dismay from
others.

Chair   The motion to introduce payment for broken
             time... is defeated!

Herbert looks gutted. Rev Marshall smiles.

Rev   Now, our task can truly begin. We shall
             sweep corruption back into the gutter... from
             whence it came. And the best place to start I
             always find... is at home.

SCENE 10
The rugby team forms once more.

Lewy   Alright lads let's keep up the standards
             we've set no matter what way the swines
             voted, we still play with all our hearts right!

The game begins. Herbert watches quietly. Reverend

Marshall stands a few feet from him, neither acknowledges the other.

There is a scream of pain at the bottom of a ruck. The cries go on but the ruck simply continues. Finally it clears to reveal George Wilkinson in agony.

Herbert   Get him sorted out, we can't hold the game up.

First aid is administered - a soaking wet rag to the back of the neck!

Gil   Cheers Florence Nightingale! Where's your lamp!?

George is carried off the pitch. Annie rushes to his side.

Annie   George! Is he alright? What's happened? George!

Lewy   Don't worry love, it's just a knock, he'll be up in a couple of minutes.

George wails in agony.

Gil   Maybe 10.

George   (*In agony*) Yeah... I'm fine, come on back in line, let's defend...

Annie   Let me see him!

Gil runs his hand over the ankle. Herbert Dalton comes to see him.

Gil	How's it feel George?
George	(*winces*) Aye… it'll be right. I'll get back on, we can't play a man down, I'll be right.
Herbert	That's it, quick rub down then back on, we've a game to win.
Lewy	Quick rub down? He's broke his leg, Mr Dalton, even I can see that!
George	(*shocked*) Gil? Lewy?
Annie	Don't panic love!

Gil and Lewy exchange glances. George looks pleadingly at Lewy, who hasn't the heart to reply.

Lewy	We need to get you to the infirmary.
George	(*furious/weeping*) Oh please not broken!
Annie	Can we get him to the infirmary or do I have to piggy back him there myself!?

George is distraught, in agony.

Annie	Don't fret George… it'll all be fine. Don't worry.

The game continues.

Herbert	Come on lads, turn and face 'em, man down or no we can win!

SCENE 11

Lewy enters. He throws his bag down. Bessie has been doing some form of tidying/re-decorating.

Bessie   Well... that's as posh a stage as I can rustle up for you. If I didn't know it before Lewy Jenkins I sure do now... this is a long way from Leicester Square!

Lewy   It's a long way from the valleys too... my old Ma and the family.

Bessie   We all have our cross to bear. Do you miss Wales?

Lewy   When the season ends we'll shut this place for a week and go down there... I'll show you the sights, oh Bessie, steam rising off mountainous slag heaps... horizontal rain like you've never seen!

Bessie   Sounds like paradise on earth! Do you promise?

Lewy   Only if you're good.

Enter Herbert Dalton.

Herbert   Am I interrupting anything?

Lewy   Mr Dalton... do come in... what brings you here?

Herbert   They're starting a witch hunt... you're just the first that's all. Hold your nerve. I've been

61

expecting it. Thought I better come and see you.

He shows Lewy a letter. Lewy's face drops. He passes the letter to her.

Bessie (*reads*) Mr Lewis Jenkins is summoned to appear before a panel of the Yorkshire Rugby Football Union, investigating allegations of... professionalism... to be chaired by Reverend Francis Marshall.

Lewy What will I do?

Herbert Don't get in a flap over it. You came here of your own accord, you've never been paid a penny.

Lewy Yeah but what if they start tying me up in knots? Hearings and that... swearing on the bible and then telling big lies, I don't...

Bessie (*in*) What do you think they do? What is it with religious types and that bible anyway?! What do any of them know about bein' poor? What people have to do to survive? They can't do anything if you hold your nerve. You look after yourself. Cos in the end, you're the only one that will.

Lewy is worried as he looks again at the letter.

Herbert Does Miss Butterworth... reside hereabouts now?

Bessie	She does indeed.
Herbert	Ah. And is Harry not miffed?
Lewy	He'll get over it.
Herbert	Aye. To get it broken, you need to actually have a heart in the first place, don't you? It's just he's the only one who could spike our tale for the Reverend… mind it's always simple with Harry, put money in his pocket… he'll do anything. Things are altering. I've had to make some decisions. Recession, recession… Prices have collapsed. There'll be folk go out of business. I won't be one of them.
Lewy	What are you going to do?
Herbert	There's two options… sack workers… thereby reducing productivity, so you make less and less money… a downward spiral.
Bessie	Or cut their wages.
Herbert	I hoped it wouldn't come to this. But it has. I've done it, by 20 per cent. It'll be the talk of the town by morning. There'll be… quite a to do about it.
Bessie	Quite a to do?
Herbert	So, Lewy, I'll need you…
Lewy	Me?! Why me?

Herbert fixes him with a steely gaze, and walks towards
him as he speaks.

Herbert   Because you're my captain... my right hand
           man on the field... we need to keep the team
           together no matter what!

Lewy   But I'm nothing to do with the mill.

Herbert   No, but the team... the team Lewy! Gil's no
           fool, same as the reverend, so we have to be
           clever. Get round all the players, tell 'em all
           there'll be 50 bob apiece for em to keep on
           playing through the strike, I'll see to it
           personally.

Lewy   20 per cent? They're gonna be angry Mr
           Dalton.

Herbert   We've got some big matches coming up, then
           a Yorkshire cup semi final!

Lewy   I really don't want to get involved.

Herbert   We are, both of us, in this together. There's
           no fence to sit on here. Between Gil and the
           Reverend, we have to watch each others
           backs and stay as one, do you understand
           me?

Lewy   (*pause*) All too well.

Herbert   Good.

Lewy	And what if they don't want to know? What then?

Herbert	They will… in time. Hunger's a terrible thing.

Lewy looks at Mr Dalton anew, shocked by the streak of steel in him.

Herbert	Do you know what sickens me? Just when we're about to win the Yorkshire Cup.

Exit Herbert. Lewy looks ashen. Bessie goes to him.

Bessie	Look… your job is to play rugby and make people happy of a Saturday… just like mine

Lewy	Exactly Bessie! It's my job… only that's against their bloody rules isn't it!

Bessie	Wage cuts, means strikes… just like Manningham in other words… Gil is…

She stops, on sight of Gil and Annie entering.

Gil	Gil is what? (*silence - no answer*) Didn't think Dalton'd be the type to drink in here, no disrespect. That is him I just saw going away, isn't it?

Lewy	Yeah.

Gil	Anything I ought to know about?

Lewy	Just… a natter… about the team.

Gil   A natter…?

Lewy   That's right. How is George? Any idea when
             he is coming home?

Annie   Not sure. Soon though. I were right looking
             forward to't bairn coming, so were George…
             now I'm wondering how we'll manage.
             Thought that were all over for us, didn't
             you? People going hungry… steady jobs,
             mills, half day off, George playing rugby,
             here you go, side of bacon, put your coat on
             we're off down the Bridge, pints of beer and
             a lemonade for her. He's never come home
             from London or any other away matches
             without bringing me somat, said he'd even
             take me to Manchester one time so I could
             look round't shops and decide what I wanted
             cos we were *never gonna be poor*, cos he'd
             always have money in his pocket. We'd go to
             Blackpool as well, stay over, bed and
             breakfast, stroll on't promenade, I said who
             do you think you are? He said *George
             Wilkinson* of *West Broughton*, little uns play
             marbles all over for my picture on a cigarette
             card and I laughed cos he were like a great
             big Cheshire cat… and now he's gonna come
             back in that door a cripple… cos his leg's
             bust in three different places and the doctor
             don't think it'll mend right and if it does he'll
             never play another game of rugby and he
             might not be able to work again either… so…
             I'd like a drink please.

She breaks entirely now, Gil goes to her.

Gil   Eh eh come on... come on... I'll... make sure
             you get treated right... you and that little
             un... I will Annie. I will. Things are
             changing... unions are starting to stand up,
             together... it in't gonna be like it was
             Annie... never again... we'll see to it... come
             what may... we'll see to it.

Lewy looks crestfallen. He looks at Bessie. Music comes in.

INTERVAL

SECOND HALF

SCENE 1

Reverend Marshall enters, takes his seat as judge of the
Inquiry hearing. A court orderly officer has a stack of
papers detailing the issues etc.

Herbert Dalton enters, followed by Bessie, then Harry
Stockwell, then Gil Gannon, and lastly Annie Wilkinson. To
the rear is George Wilkinson.

Finally, when all are assembled and ready Lewy Jenkins
enters. Lewy stares at Rev Marshall, who returns it with
interest for a few seconds.

Rev M   It falls to me to chair this hearing, on behalf
               of the Yorkshire Rugby Football Union, to
               investigate the precise nature of Mr Lewis
               Jenkins tenure to West Broughton Rugby
               Football Club. We seek to establish whether
               any inducement was paid, in cash or in kind,
               to persuade Mr Jenkins to break faith with
               his former club and render his services not
               only to West Broughton, but the *licensed
               victuallers* trade also. Make no mistake, we
               are fighting here for the soul of the game. No
               matter what form remuneration to players
               might take... it is professionalism. It will
               destroy this game and leave us with nothing
               but a band of itinerant mercenaries who care
               nothing for the noble sport of rugby and
               everything for themselves and their own
               pocket. Now, do you swear before Almighty
               God to tell the truth Mr Jenkins?

Lewy   (*pause*) I do.

Rev	(*gently*) Very good. Now, do you understand the charges that have been brought against you?
Lewy	Yes.
Rev M	And what do you say to them?
Lewy	(*nervous*) I... I... didn't... deny them.
Rev	Really? You don't deny them? This is good...
Lewy	No no sir I mean do... I deny them.
Rev	Mr Jenkins... please... which is it to be? I am fully aware that other people may have put you...
Lewy	(*in*) I deny them Reverend.
Rev	Then pray tell how exactly did you come to move here? Who proposed the move to you exactly?
Lewy	No-one did.
Rev	No-one? Come now. A coalminer, one who has lived his entire life in South Wales, doubtless seldom strayed more than a stones throw from his birthplace, acted on a whim to move to an area where you know nobody, for no reason at all?
Lewy	That... that is what I did Reverend yes.

Rev	I beg your pardon, can you speak up please.
Lewy	That's the truth of it Reverend.
Rev	I doubt that somehow.
Lewy	Look… it was clear as a bell to me that the Yorkshire and Lancashire teams were by far the best in the country. I consider myself to be among the best players in the country so I decided I wanted to play at the highest level that I could.
Rev	So you joined a team which had not won a game for several weeks prior to your arrival?
Lewy	They were kind enough to welcome me with open arms and it's always nice to feel needed.
Rev	The Red Lion Inn. I believe a deposit has to be placed with the owners of any public house in order to secure the tenancy. How much was that sum?
Lewy	It was… it was £50.
Rev	50 pounds?
Lewy	Yes.
Rev	A fair sum. And prior to taking up said tenancy, you were employed as a coalminer.
Lewy	That's correct.

Rev	Who swore before the Almighty to tell the truth. You are a Christian Mr Jenkins.
Lewy	Yes. I am Reverend.
Rev	Very good. What is the weekly wage of a coalminer?
Lewy	(*pause*) 21 shillings.
Rev	21 shillings? From which you must feed and keep yourself.
Lewy	That's correct.
Rev	How then, did you come by the sum of 50 pounds?
Lewy	(*pause*) I... I...
Herbert	He saved it.
Rev	Mr Jenkins, God is watching... he hears our every word, every thought. Think very carefully. I shall be able to exercise some leniency if you drop this pathetic tissue of lies, and tell the truth and shame the devil. Well? What is it to be?

Lewy pauses, breathes deeply, all eyes upon him.

Lewy	I worked very hard and I saved... most of it.
Rev	Most of it? How did you come by the remainder?

Lewy   I... my dear old Ma was always very good
            with money and she gave me her life savings
            to help set me up.

Lewy's Ma & old teacher, Mr Griffiths appear now, at the
edges of the scene – as if in his consciousness. Gradually
the scene morphs from the hearing to the following one in
the Red Lion.

Ma   Knees and elbows my darling Lewy... don't
            let them catch you.

Rev   So be it. You have made your pact. Please
            Mr Jenkins... I offer you one last opportunity
            to unburden your soul... to consider the
            greater picture... your responsibility to the
            young, and impressionable, who follow you
            so avidly, who cheer you from the terraces
            and hold you in such high esteem.

Teacher   Oh it's Lewy this and Lewy that. All they
            ever ask me about is you... it's a gift from
            God Lewy... you're everything to them see.
            What they dream of every night, when their
            head hits the pillow... imagine that eh? A
            hero on the field... one they'll never forget...
            whatever else, don't come home a fool Lewy.
            Don't do that to them. That'd be terrible.

Lewy   I take my responsibility to them very
            seriously! And what's more I have done
            nothing wrong, alright?!

Ma   I don't care what you've done... I'm so proud
            of you... and your Da would be too.

Lewy	Would he? Would he though?
Teacher	Just don't come home a fool.
Lewy	Look I'm doing everything I can damn it why won't they let me be..?

SCENE 2

The scene switches to the Red Lion. Lewy wakes with a jolt.

Bessie	Lewy! Lewy calm.
Lewy	What!? Where am I!?
Bessie	You're dreaming sweetheart.
Lewy	What am I gonna do Bessie? What am I gonna tell the Reverend and his inquiry, eh? It's alright for Mr Dalton he's dealt with stuff like this but I never have!
Bessie	Lewy, in for a penny... the Reverend will ask you loads of questions and so long as you keep your nerve it'll be fine. Now, remember what Mr Dalton said? The players are supposed to be here soon and they need you to speak, to lead them
Lewy	Where the hell are they then?
Bessie	Calm yourself, they'll be here.
Lewy	And then what? What'll I say to 'em? Hello lads, Mr Dalton wants you all to know how

much he cares about you… that's why he's just cut your wages, but please stay and play for the team and he'll make it up to you on the side you know.

Bessie   Sounds alright if you ask me, swings and roundabouts, that's life.

Lewy   Not how Gil sees it. Where are they then? I told them all to meet here at 7.

Enter Annie, helping George.

Lewy   George, how you doing mate?

George   Right enough.

Annie   Exactly, I've entered him in a one legged race, so he needn't think it's all sitting on his backside like Lord muck from here on.

George   (*terse*) I don't.

Bessie   Where's the bairn this evening?

Annie stops dead.

Annie   Do you know, I knew I'd forgotten something! Oh he can't o' gone far, he'll turn up.

George   He's at Annie's mams. Are you serving any beer in this pub.

Annie   Alright George… no need to be snapping.

George	Well… what's up Lewy?
Lewy	Eh? Oh, nothing… Yet. I called a players meeting for 7… it's near 25 past and no sign of them.

Annie sees George flinch at that.

Annie	Players meeting… what for if you don't mind my enquiring?
Lewy	To talk… team stuff.
Annie	What team stuff?
George	It isn't any of our business now Annie.
Lewy	To… have a word with them that's all.
Annie	To butter 'em up with a few bob and the odd leg of lamb, to go on playing is that it? Keep his team rolling on?
George	Annie!
Annie	And everything sunny side up for Dalton, while he cuts their mates wages, and we can't afford dry bread, while they're out on strike, but the rugby players will look after theirselves and blow everyone else?
Lewy	Annie don't get involved, lads don't like it, team stuff is between players and…
Annie	So come on what is he offering em?

George	Annie!
Annie	Seeing as they're not here you tell me and I'll get round em.
Lewy	There'll be 50 bob for every man who turns out on Saturday.
Annie	Right… well that's a tidy sum to people with nothing isn't it.
Bessie	Exactly. What would you have done George? In their shoes? Offered money? Hard cash when… you've a family… they have a right to feed theirs don't they?
Annie	They won't take it.
Bessie	And how do you know that? Who said you speak for em all?
Annie	Because I know 'em. Not if Gil says not to. You don't understand 'em like I do… maybe they would in Wales… I don't suppose you've ever took a stand over right and wrong either…
Bessie	Don't you?
Annie	But here going on strike, means that.
Bessie	Easy for you to say. It's not like George has any choice to make is it?
Annie	I know the one he'd make if he had.

George	Aye. I'd have took it. I'd have played.
Annie	No you would not!
George	Yes I would have! And not a second thought.
Annie	(*hurt*) You would not have and don't say different!
Lewy	Look let's not bring George into this, it's been hard enough on him, whatever happens we look after each other, you're still one of us.
George	Aye. I appreciate that.
Lewy	Now, let's have a drink and stop this…
George	After all he's no use to anyone now so what's the point in bringing him into it?
Lewy	I didn't mean that bloody hell! Please George… let's not turn on each other.
George	No. 50 bob for every man who plays eh?

Enter Gil.

Gil	And a black mark by his name that he'll never wash off as long as he lives.
Lewy	They're entitled to make their own minds up.
Gil	That they are.

George	50 bob'll come in handy Gil.
Gil	I know it will. But in times to come everyone'll know who stood firm, and who looked after himself. Won't be many kids running after 'em in't street then will there? Eh Lewy? Worth thinking about.
Lewy	Every man has the right to make his own mind up. They didn't get the broken time vote through and that's that.
Gil	Broken time give me strength! Rabbits don't vote for the pot. You never thought they'd bring that in did you? You side with Dalton if you want. But I know the only way to deal with him is to make him suffer... see how he likes it, take his toys off him.

Enter Herbert. All bristle and stiffen up on sight of him.

Herbert	Evening all.
Annie	Oh my giddy aunt! All here that means owt now eh, where's the Reverend and we've a full house.
George	Annie!
Herbert	Annie. Gilbert. I thought I'd call in for a pint and catch a bit o' banter. George... are you alright lad?
George	Not so bad thanks Mr Dalton.

Herbert	Good lad. Keep your chin up. I'll find a job for you somewhere... don't worry.
George	Thanks very much I appreciate it.
Herbert	Get your leg back so you can get about on it, you'll be able to come and help out with the team on Saturdays, still be involved and that.
George	Thank you sir.

Annie looks from George to Herbert, amazed at how George just folded.

Annie	What? Is that all you're gonna say to him?
George	Let Gil speak to him.
Annie	Why do you need Gil to speak...? What's the matter with you that you can't look him in the eye yourself and...
George	Just be quiet will you! Shuttup! Right? Just... let Gil deal with it, it's nowt to do with us any more, Mr Dalton has important things to deal with and he don't need the likes of you in his earhole any more than I flaming well do like a bloody insect buzzing round me yap yap all the bloody time!
Annie	George?
George	I'm sorry Mr Dalton, Lewy. Annie and I are going home.

Annie	Are we?
George	Fine… you do as you like. I can't tell you no more can I? I don't want to be here.

He gets up and makes his way out. Annie is heartbroken.

Annie	What am I gonna do, Gil? Every night I pray it'll end, I'll wake up and have him back… as he was.
Bessie	He'll come round, be his old self again.
Annie	I hope so. I better go.

She exits. There is a heavy pause, no-one speaks for a while.

Herbert	He's lost everything that matters to him… the thing he lived and breathed God's good air for, taken away from him.
Gil	He in't the first it's happened to, won't be the last.
Herbert	Are you really gonna do this? Take the players on flaming strike just when we're turning into the best team in the country?
Gil	Not down to me Mr Dalton. The fellers make their own choices. I just dropped by to tell Lewy what they said. Well Lewy… what's it to be? Whose side are you on?
Lewy	It's not that simple. For all we get paid… under the counter or over… it's still a game

	we love to play, it can't just be… another way of fighting politics and all that.
Gil	Why not? There's a lot more to life than rugby. Good Welsh mining boy like you, what was it? "trade unions no bad thing"… I heard you say it. Well? Are you one of us… or a crawling lackey?
Lewy	You watch what you say.
Herbert	Easy now lads.
Gil	I told you be careful who your friends are… us or them Lewy… there's no in between… that's how it is.
Lewy	I never felt we made it as far as friends. I'm pretty choosy in that area.
Gil	So are folk round here… boot licking toady's don't last long.
Lewy	I warned you once and I won't again!
Herbert	Now now boys keep it civil.
Gil	He made you captain, put you in here, filled your pockets… and why? So you'd be his… bought and paid for…
Lewy	I told you shut it!

Lewy lunges for Gil, Herbert gets in between them.

Bessie	Fellas for God's sake! Mr Dalton stop them!
Herbert	Come on now lads finish it outside in't yard if you need to, but you'll only be a laughing stock, all of us right and proper! Word gets out the best two players in the team at each others throats! We have to keep the strike and the rugby separate.
Gil	You do. I don't.
Herbert	We all flamin' do! This town is the team, and same the other way. Don't cut your nose off to spite your face. We lost the broken time vote... but there's move afoot. Things are altering... I've spoken to other chairmen all across Yorkshire and Lancashire... they're all in the same boat as me... let's be clear about one thing, them in London are trying to skewer the game up here, cos we knock hell out of em, they can't hold a candle to the northern teams cos of lads like you. And they've an ally in the Reverend and all the other *gentlemen* from these parts because they don't want mill lads and miners lads like you rubbing shoulders on equal terms with em... it puts their noses right out and thats the top and bloody bottom of it! Right! Now we three in here are all on't same damn side can't you see it!? That's what the buggers care about! Not flamin amateurism at all, but if they get their way enforce it on us it'll put this game back thirty years...nay flaming destroy it up here. That's what they want! But I won't let em. One day, not far off, we'll

get a straight up and proper way of paying you, for broken time, but who knows where it could go? We'll have the best game in the world, and West Broughton'll be the best payers in it. You'll earn more from rugby than you'd ever see on a mill floor, more than you can spend at Blackpool in a week. But we need to stick together now. I'm asking you once again and once only, play on Saturday.

Gil
God's honest? I'd love to. Nothing makes me happier than a good game... the harder the better, nothing to touch it... when your lungs are busting, your eyes bloodshot swollen up so you can scarce see... your head hurts, arms, neck, shoulders, every bone in your body's on fire wi' pain,

Lewy
But you get up, get back in line, defend... because the bloke next to you needs you...

Gil
Because the crowd are willing you on and you ride that wave of... feeling, emotion, it lifts you on to do things you never knew you could do... your team mates don't need to speak... one look between you says it... we're a good side... we're a proud side... we'll not be beat today...

Herbert
Aye. And ten thousand souls up in them stands... get more from that... than any other thing in their lives! That's what a team, a club, a *town* is... Gil please lad, I'll pay you damn well! I don't care, put it in your pocket

and bring 'em all back! The Yorkshire Cup! What have we aimed to win for the last five years!? It's the biggest competition in the land!

Gil slowly shakes his head.

Gil   Keep your money. I'd play for nothing to bring that cup back here, see everyone's faces.

Herbert   Well then! Eh?

Gil   But if I run out there on Saturday, everyone'll know we've had another backhander to do it. And they'll all think the same thing… we're all hungry… stood in lines for soup kitchens… and that Gil Gannon, us union feller, he just looked after himself. You see, if I didn't know it before I do now, rugby's a lot more than just a game these days.

Herbert   Gilbert… I'm asking you… begging you.

Gil   No wage cut?

Herbert   I can't alter that.

Gil   Like I said Lewy. You've got to decide which side you're on. Well, I'll get off… oh… near forgot… I got a letter this morning as well… asking me to attend an investigative hearing in a couple of weeks time as well.

Bessie   You wouldn't do that… would you?

84

Gil	Wouldn't I? I look forward to resuming our negotiations, Mr Dalton, regarding the unfortunate business of the wage 'restructuring' as recently implemented by the management of Dalton & Sons. Night to you both, wrap up warm going home, there's a very chill wind blowing.
Herbert	There bloody well is.

He exits. Herbert is gutted, Lewy scared.

Lewy	Mr Dalton... this is all getting very nasty now.
Herbert	I told you it would. He's an hard swine. Link the strike up with the rugby... He thinks he has me.
Lewy	What do you mean *you* Mr Dalton? Us both!
Herbert	That's what I meant, aye course it is.
Lewy	It's okay for you, but... I just want to do better, for myself, and the team, that's all... what if I'm banned? What then? No public house, Harry'll bounce me out of here in two seconds won't he?
Herbert	Harry won't do a blind thing while you've got me behind you, don't fret an eyelid about that. You'll go before that hearing and say nowt, do you hear me? The Reverend'll ask you time and again, you tell him you know nowt, saw nowt, heard nowt... you just keep

85

	on playing and I'll see you right, no matter what.
Lewy	Yeah. Me keep on doing your bidding.
Herbert	Leather soled shoes and hand stitched waistcoats, you're very own Lily Langtree on your arm. You have it good. Just remember who gave it you.

Lewy looks distraught. Herbert exits.

Lewy	What am I gonna do Bess? I can't… I can't go back to the pit… not now… not after this… big crowds cheering… money in my pocket. I can't go back.

In comes the brass band.

SCENE 3

Matchday, the board reads **WEST BROUGHTON versus HUDDERSFIELD – Yorkshire Cup semi final, Saturday March 5th, 1894**.

Enter the gents only team. Lewy stands inspecting his teammates.

Lewy	Gather round lads, now we lost last week, and the one before.
Fro	But I seriously think we are making improvements Mr Jenkins.
Lewy	I quite agree Mr Frobisher, just not enough quick enough. And er Mr Frobisher…

Fro	Mr Jenkins?

Lewy	It's called tackling not tickling.

Enter the umpire in his bowler hat, cigar in mouth. The game gets underway.

Herbert enters, Rev Marshall and finally Harry Stockwell. The sound of the game and some form of stylised rugby sequence occurs on the field. Bessie arrives to watch the game. She sees Harry and looks away.

Harry	Blimey have we a semi final on today or is it a funeral? Seen more excitement at one of your sermons Reverend.

Rev	The working players appear to have absented themselves? Bar one. How very churlish. Nothing could further strengthen my point. They have no sense of what sport is.

Harry	Getting thrashed on your own field?

Rev	Their minds have been debased… they see their toil on the rugby field as no more than any other transaction, of labour spent in return for reward. I trust you'll stand firm in the face of this intimidation. You can rely upon my full support, I shall amend my sermon accordingly.

Harry	I can hardly wait.

Rev	I beg your pardon?

Harry	Nothing.
Herbert	They're being used, by a devious clever swine, who'll lead us all to wrack and ruin, Reverend.
Rev	I disagree entirely. One day soon those of us who cherish this game will see it returned to us.
Herbert	Nobody loves this game more than me. Or the crowds that used to be here when we had a team worth watching!
Rev	Those of us who understand it's true nature will see it returned to it's pure form, it's true place within a just and ordered society.
Herbert	Hasn't the transaction of labour in return for reward got a place in a just and ordered society Reverend?
Rev	It has a place. But you people put it above all else. Look at the towns and cities you have left us with. You build grand monuments to yourselves, but on what foundations? All around them are cesspits of filth, vice, avarice, greed and sickness of every hue. That is *your* West Broughton... a horrible dirty place... I see it with my own eyes... that is your true legacy Mr Dalton... and it's the reason I so utterly despise you.
Herbert	If you weren't a churchman I'd knock your block off for saying that.

Rev	And if you and your kind weren't so bloated on your own wealth and importance this game would be free of the poison you pour through its veins.
Herbert	Oh... getting personal are we?
Rev	This game is the heartbeat of an Englishman's character. Sport prepares young men for life ahead, service, duty, diligence and self sacrifice. To serve and further the empire, bring Christianity and civilization to the heathen far and wide. These are the values of all good schools. Young men's physical prowess and skill on the field is a gift from God, and ought be used for his glorification and the service of others.
Herbert	What are you talking about man? The queues of people at the turnstile haven't come to see anyone prepare to defend the empire! They've come for an afternoon out, entertainment! A good bawl at the umpire. We're talking about two different things entirely man. Worlds apart.

Herbert exits. Harry Stockwell looks on surprised.

Harry	Well, I can't say for certain, Reverend, but I think you've upset him.
Rev	(*grins widely*) I have scarcely begun. You are a man of the world Harry... I... think sometimes I am out of step with...

Harry	With reality?
Rev	Oh no… not that… not at all. My reality is different from his that's all. With the times perhaps. But just because the times change… fashions alter, one cannot abandon one's… beliefs… principles.
Harry	I admire a man with principles. I just admire a man with money that bit more.
Rev	I'm sure you have some conscience somewhere.
Harry	(*thinks*) No… Somewhere. Maybe.
Rev	What if I were to test your resolve? What if I were to ask you to attend the hearing into Mr Jenkins arrangement with our club.
Harry	Oh I wouldn't know anything about that.
Rev	Yes you would, since it was you who brokered the whole arrangement… was it not?
Harry	Mr Dalton's been a good friend, put a lot of business my way down the years. I could never betray his trust. It would… go against my principles, and I never break a principle…
Rev	I quite understand.
Harry	Unless I stand to benefit, what exactly are you offering?

Rev	A place on the Yorkshire RFU committee? In the event you showed your colours in defence of the amateur... ideal.
Harry	A place on the Yorkshire Committee?
Rev	Very prestigious.
Harry	Well, to serve the game as a whole... in a dutiful and diligent manner, no matter what the sacrifice to myself, would be the... ultimate enactment of my principles, Reverend.
Rev	That is very gratifying to hear. It will bring you into some very powerful circles.
Harry	I don't doubt. It's just that, in the event I told your committee anything, it'd land me in as much bother as Lewy and Dalton. Wouldn't it? Which would defeat the object.
Rev	The sinner who repents is the same in God's eyes as he who has lived without blemish.
Harry	That's nice but it's the RFU's eyes I'm worried about.
Rev	I give you my word, deliver Jenkins and the corruption at the heart of the West Broughton club to me... and I shall see to it you are personally exonerated and thanked for telling the truth finally.
Harry	Why are you worked up about all this Reverend?

Rev	The game… I care merely what is good and right for the game.
Harry	Really?
Rev	Yes. Really. I have loved sport all my life. But more than that, each day I see those boys at Almondbury School, 20 years from now they will be our leaders, our captains… they must know true values, honour, valour, in a new century. I think of the world we shall bequeath them… it is improved in many ways… I have nothing against machines that make people's lives easier or better… but there are values beyond that.
Harry	And you believe in these sacred principles so much… that you're willing to bribe me for them.
Rev	Good heavens no.

Enter Lewy.

Lewy	Where's Mr…
Rev	Jenkins.
Lewy	Hello.
Rev	Come to claim your illicit booty no doubt? Not for long young man. Not for long.

Exit the Reverend.

Lewy	Where's Dalton?
Harry	He went home. Couldn't bear to watch it.
Lewy	I know how he feels. That is the worst 15 I ever played in. I didn't come here to be made to look a fool.
Harry	It's not what I had in mind when I came to Wales to find you neither. You might cut a mean stride on the field son... but off it I don't think you know quite what you're up against.
Lewy	Is that a fact?

Harry gets suddenly passionate, nasty.

Harry	I have a very... powerful attachment... to that girl! You put my nose out of joint and, make a mug of me, I'll have you back on your belly in that pit before you can say scrum down, no hacking, gouging, spitting, punching or farting. Do I make myself clear?
Lewy	Crystal. But Harry... know this my friend... if I was to put your nose out of joint... you wouldn't know about it for at least a day and a half... do I make myself clear?

Lewy turns to exit.

Harry	You were warned.
Lewy	(*sharp/angry*) And? What of it? What are you

gonna do Harry? Go before the Reverend
and do me in would you? I don't think Mr
Dalton will like that.

Harry   Who do you think you have to thank for
             this!? It was my idea to bring you here! And
             what thanks do I get? She was mine damn it!

Lewy   Aye... just another bit of property you and
             Dalton can have and own... well maybe not
             this time eh?

Harry   No... no... you don't understand... it's not
             that at all. (*pause*) But I don't have to explain
             myself to you.

Lewy   No. That's not how it works is it. Well, she's
             made her bed.

Harry   Aye... and so have you.

Lewy exits. Harry stares after him.

SCENE 4
Lewy enters the Red Lion. Bessie is there.

Bessie   You got stuffed. What a bunch of old Aunt
             sally's! Big prancin' pansies. Not even a
             proper full steam, up and at 'em, 30 man
             punch up!

Lewy   Thank you. Believe it or not Bessie
             afternoons like that... are very hard to take
             for a man like me.

Bessie	They're not much cop to a girl like me neither, stood freezing me aunt mary's off... oh well, it's only a game.
Lewy	It bloody well is not! If I didn't know that before, I surely do now. Now Harry's trying to threaten me... over you... Gil the same... and they can all dob me in to the Reverend.
Bessie	That Gil's another one just like Harry and Dalton, all out for himself.
Lewy	No he isn't, he's out for his own people... and I'm stuck on the wrong side of this row. How can I side with a man who cuts people's wages? What I hate the most... is that I am Mr Dalton's man, bought and paid for, he paid for the tenancy on this place... gave me money to sign on... owns me lock stock. The one thing I wanted when I got out of the pit... freedom... I haven't got that at all have I? And if they ban me from playing... that's it isn't it? Back to Wales... looking a bloody fool, back on my belly. I won't be able to play for the local team like before. I'll be finished, thrown out... with a pick... finish up like my Da.
Bessie	Then stand up for pity's sake! Think! People in this town worship you! They won't let Gil stab you in the back, they won't forgive him if he does.
Lewy	He's right though isn't he? I am Dalton's lackey.

Bessie	You are your own man… and when you go before the reverend you look him square in the eye and you tell him you bought your own tenancy with your own money and you play rugby cos you love it and you've never had a penny out of it… have you now?
Lewy	No… course not. So now I'm not just a mercenary… I'm a strikebreaking scab and a liar before God himself.
Bessie	Don't let them scare you.
Lewy	All this for a game of rugby! Great. Look at what they do… turn you into a criminal, and a liar. I am deep in it now Bessie.
Bessie	You need to think clever, about yourself… like Dalton'd give a fig about you if you bust your leg like George, blow him, the Reverend, Gil Gannon… and God as well if he makes folk into liars and cheats!
Lewy	Now steady on Bessie that's… not good talk!
Bessie	You're the best of 'em all. And if I didn't know that before… I do now. We need to think.
Lewy	I love you Bessie. I love this little town… it's nothing of a place… but I like it here. I just wanna play… earn a living… same as anybody else.
Bessie	I know. People here love you… we need

them to see you really care about them…
what they're going through.

Lewy   Oh. How?

Bessie   People are hungry, kids stood at soup
            kitchens, they need you.

Lewy   What am I gonna do?

Bessie   You're going to stage one of them special
            fundraising rugby match. With the very best
            stars of the game, from far and wide, all
            lending their brotherly support to the
            striking textile workers!

Lewy   Am I?

Bessie   Oh yes. With half time entertainment
            provided by popular music hall artistes… a
            little sprinkle of Bessie magic you might say!

Lewy   Might I?

Bessie   We, you I mean, could make it like a big
            family day out… music, songs, dancing girls
            on the pitch at half time, a brass band…

Lewy   Singing? Dancing girls on the pitch? People
            at rugby matches won't go for all that
            razzamatazz!

Bessie   Course they will!

Lewy   I don't think so. Not in Yorkshire Bessie,
            they're not that type.

Bessie	They'll love it! We'll have games for the kiddies and mascots in costumes, everything! It'll raise a fortune, make all the newspapers, and everyone'll see what a smashing chap you are! People will cheer you louder than ever. Gil won't dare stab you in the back, neither will Harry and Dalton can stick it in his pipe and smoke it.

Lewy gazes at her awestruck.

Lewy	Wow!
Bessie	I know. I'll go far. You see I know these swines… you need to play smart… (*taps her head*) up here.
Lewy	Just like on the pitch. Are they gonna smash us up the middle or try and play round the side of us.
Bessie	Exactly, but the smart team does both, just when you're expecting one, wam bam, they hit you with the other.
Lewy	Are you sure you've never played rugby?
Bessie	Sweetheart… this is what you need to get in that big fine head of yours… there's games way, way, tougher than rugby.
Lewy	I don't think I'm cut out for them.
Bessie	It's why I'm here. Stick with me Welsh boy.

Lewy	Oh I very powerfully intend to. People here love me? I need one in particular... to love me.
Bessie	You are a good man Lewy... I never thought...
Lewy	Tell me... do you?
Bessie	(*pause/surprised*) Yes... I do...

He takes hold of her, pullss her to him.

Lewy	I'm not scared of nothing!
Bessie	Then me neither! Now, we need some players and some turns, dancing girls all of it, you get the players I'll get the rest. Chop chop!

Music - the full brass section.

SCENE 5

Harry enters the main stand area, to see Herbert.

Herbert	All Star Benefit match my big fat Yorkshire behind!
Harry	You won't be buying a raffle ticket then? I didn't expect to see you here Mr Dalton.
Herbert	My flaming rugby ground isn't it? Bloody cheek!

Harry	Aye... our lion of the valleys just doesn't twig where his bread's buttered does he?

Music plays – Bessie enters. The All Star match is about to begin. Across the stage George Wilkinson enters, sits alone. Bessie lists the players.

Bessie	Ladies and gentleman thank you all for attending today... we're lucky to have some of the greatest stars of the rugby world with us today, the outstanding half back James Wright! The dashing George Marsden!
Herbert	The hearing is tomorrow. Lewy's frightened you'll dob him into the reverend, over Miss Butterworth.
Harry	Oh I have no thought for myself, merely the good of the game you understand, Herbert.
Herbert	Harry don't play both sides with me. You're up to you're neck in skulduggery same as I am, they'll drum you out of the game as quick as Lewy.
Harry	Won't help your own standing much either will it.
Herbert	So we all need to mind each others' backs don't we?
Harry	Aye. Don't we. I have a letter... it came from London just this morning... concerning Miss Butterworth.

Herbert   Oh? Saying what?

Harry produces the letter.

Harry   "Dear Mr Stockwell,
Please accept my sincerest felicitations and
may I say how gaily my heart sang to hear
from you, a rising giant of the music hall
stage in the far parts of the kingdom…"

Herbert   Bloody theatricals.

Harry   "However I beg forbearance, please kind sire
forgive my verbosity for it is with regard to
your most divine, boundlessly gifted Miss
Bessie Butterworth that I now pen this
humble missive…

Herbert   Get on with it.

Harry   "the stage at The Empire Theatre, Leicester
Square, London, most eagerly awaits her
presence."

Herbert   So?

Harry   If she goes… I don't think Lewy will be too
far behind.

Herbert   Oh I see.

Harry   Now if I could… engineer a situation where
Miss Butterworth was unable to take up their
kind offer, for whatever reason.

Herbert	I'd be very grateful.
Bessie	All the way from sunny Heckmondwike, the much travelled, legend of the modern game, Mr Dickie Lockwood! Mr Jack Toothill! Followed by the one and only Arthur 'Spafty' Briggs! Last but not least, from Wales, the one the only, our very own Lewy Jenkins!! And finally Mr Gilbert Gannon!
Herbert	I need to end this strike and now. It's my mill. I need to get it working again. Strike or no.
Harry	You mean...?
Herbert	Aye... scab labour. That's what I mean.

The game kicks in. George is alone. Annie comes to him now.

George	Dickie Lockwood, George Marsden... Jack Toothill, Spafty Briggs. Played agin 'em all... good players... good lads.
Annie	George Wilkinson! The biggest name of all. To me anyway.
George	Aye. Just not to anyone else.
Annie	You've got to accept it now... and learn to laugh again... you were always laughing before. It's like my Ma used to say...
George	Laugh and the world...?

Annie   No, straighten that face afore I straighten it for you you skivvy little nowt, now gerrout and fetch some coal, then scrub these spuds afore I flail the skin off you!

George   (*shocked*) Did she?

Annie   (*smiling, gentle*) But we always knew she loved us really.

George looks unconvinced.

George   Right… I'm just glad she didn't love me.

Annie   She would have. She'd have belted you for drinking and gambling though.

George   I reckon so.

Annie jumps up suddenly.

Annie   Go on Dickie Lockwood! What a player! Did you see that!?

George   Aye… I did.

He looks at Annie, as she is completely absorbed in the game. He puts his arm around her, pulls her close, her head goes to his shoulder.

In come the sound of drums in the distance, with a military beat. They get slowly, steadily louder.

Herbert   I've arranged a new workforce to come and operate the machines.

Harry	That won't sit too well will it?
Herbert	They'll forget, in time, especially if we've a team the envy of the land. With Lewy Jenkins in it, who knows maybe Dickie Lockwood too… imagine them two side by side.
Harry	It'd take some beating.
Herbert	It would. So I want you to end your little spat with Lewy, and burn that letter from London… just to make it all easier for you… I'm going to give you a seat in the board of the rugby club, on top of that there's other deals I can bring you in on… land deals and property, I'm going to be building houses Harry, lots of em, then a school, then hospital, a library… who knows, in a few years they might think better of me. Might even get me own statue, what do you think? Just like Titus Salt has in Bradford.
Harry	Who knows. Though personally I can't applaud a man who builds a village with no pub in it. but there we are.
Herbert	I went to his funeral, pulled hell of a crowd he did… (*suddenly Herbert shudders/afraid almost*) it's just that he died with scarcely a penny to his name, did you know that? They don't talk about that do they?
Harry	No. Rest assured Mr Dalton… the reverend won't hear a peep out of me.

SCENE 6

The hearing re- forms.

Rev   Mr Gannon, thank you very much for your prompt reply to my letter and I would be very grateful if you could join us here.

Gil steps forward, nods casually to Herbert and Lewy.

Rev   You were leader of the Weavers Union during the recent unfortunate strike action at Dalton's Mill, as well as being leader of the working players within the West Broughton team, prior to the strike, is that fair?

Gil   No. He made Lewy captain.

Rev   Why was that?

Gil   Ask him.

Rev   You and Mr Jenkins were not the closest of friends during your time together on the team?

Gil   Who told you that?

Rev   You were unhappy at his arrival at the club?

Gil   No.

Rev   Especially when he was promoted to the role of captain ahead of you?

Gil	Rough with the smooth Reverend.
Rev	You were one of the finest players on the team for many years.
Gil	Good of you to say so.
Rev	A leader, on the field and off.
Gil	If you say.
Rev	It must have been a trifle galling to see the broohaha which surrounded Mr Jenkins upon his arrival at the club? Installed as landlord of the Red Lion Inn when no such arrangement had been made for you, promoted to captain within days of his arrival? Is this why you led the players revolt? What prompted that?
Gil	The strike caused everyone to take sides… feelings were running high.
Rev	Talking the players round to withdrawing from the team, must have cost them all a great deal?
Gil	(*pause*) Some people care about more than money. I just tried to… explain that to Lewy.
Rev	Mr Gannon, as an avowed trade unionist, you take the view that a man ought be paid fairly for his endeavours I presume?
Gil	I do.

Rev	Be that in any sphere of life?
Gil	I hold to the view that rugby players ought be compensated for broken time at work, if that's what you're referring to.
Rev	Mr Gannon did you withdraw the working players from the team because of bitterness caused by the industrial unrest… or jealousy that Mr Jenkins was being *paid*, while you were not? Did Mr Jenkins not continue to play during that unrest simply because he was a waged employee of Mr Dalton on the rugby field?

The drum returns.

Gil	I've had my run in's with Lewy… and any issue I have I'll take up with him. But I'll not jump to for you Reverend… put an even playing field down for lads like us and I might care what you think… I have nothing more to add. I know nothing about any payments ever made to anyone by anyone and I don't believe there is any.
Rev	I see. That will be all.

Lewy looks over at Gil and nods in appreciation. Mutual respect.

Gil	In fact I might form a players union… seems to me players like us need proper formal representation in the face of these bullying, intimidatory tactics.

As Gil steps down and returns to his seat Herbert turns to Lewy winks boldly at him. Then he turns to Gil.

Herbert   Thanks a lot Gilbert, I appreciate it.

Gil   I won't betray a bloke I played beside, that's all. But you... I wouldn't spit on you if you were on fire.

Gil exits. Herbert turns his gaze to the Reverend, who is very dismayed.

SCENE 7
Bessie is alone when Harry approaches her.

Harry   Hello sweetpea.

She doesn't reply, watches him warily.

Harry   I hear you did well... you and Lewy put on a very grand do. The very best, playing for the best of good folks.

Bessie   I'm so glad you approve.

Harry   Does Lewy know you only did it to spite me?

Bessie   No... because it's not why *we* did it... me and Lewy... he's a good man.

Harry   Unlike me. (*pause*) And it raised a few quid, no-one'd deny 'em that. But now it's time to come home Bess... to me. I love you. I don't know why you don't see that.

Bess	I do… I've had the bruises to prove it.

Harry	(*pause*) I got a letter… from London.

Pause. She looks at him, waiting for him to explain further.

Harry	(*pause*) How do you think it's going to end… this strike?

Bessie	I don't know. At least they'll be able to look themselves in the eye.

Harry	You don't think old Dalton's gonna risk his empire just cos his rugby team goes to the devil do you? These wool barons and kings of Industry… they know what they're doing alright, they get what they want, and they don't care how they how they get it.

He hands her the letter.

	Open it.

Bessie	You helped me Harry, and I won't forget it.

She opens the letter and reads.

The drums return, this time they get louder. As Harry speaks the rest of the cast come onto the stage. They form, into lines facing one another. Harry and Bessie are in a separate reality from this.

Harry	There'll be police, then scab labour, and soldiers, oh aye, some on horseback… I did more than damn well help you!

She looks up from the letter, the implications of it dawning on her.

Gil   Here we go... stand together we knew it was coming.

George   Let em come! It'll take somat to break this back line eh Gil?

Bessie   Yes you did... The Empire Theatre Leicester Square... on the bill with Marie Lloyd?! I'm dreaming!?

Harry   No angel... it's all real... we're lucky... you and me... our boat is about to come in alright.

Bessie   What do you mean?

Harry   Read the letter sweetpea... that is the number one stage in this country... requesting your presence... that is big time serious money we always dreamed of...

Bessie   Harry I...

Harry   We're lucky you and me.

Annie   George!

Bessie   You and I...

George   Go home Annie... nowt to worry about... we'll sort this out and be home in time for tea. Eh Gil, where's that Wagstaff from't paper now eh? We could give him a quote now couldn't we!?

Bessie   (*pause*) What are you doing Harry?

Harry   So... the strikers will stand their ground will they? And the soldiers'll read out the riot act, loud and clear.

A section of the riot act is read here:

"Our Sovereign Queen chargeth all persons being here assembled to disperse themselves and peaceably depart to their habitations..."

Harry   You need to remember who your friends really are.

Bessie   Harry? You can't make me love you!

Now Harry looks at her, slowly shakes his head. The drums keep coming.

Annie   Gil! Stop him! He in't fit to fight em!

Gil   Let him be... he's one of us... front row now same as always always in't you George.

Harry   But them strikers... they won't give in... they can't... they've staked their caps to it you see. They think they have a choice.

Bessie   No-one should be a piece of meat belonging to someone else!

Harry	And after a while when the soldiers see that pushing and shoving only gets 'em so far... there'll be one last chance...
Soldier	By order of the Crown you are hereby to disperse this place and return to your homes, or my men will be ordered to open fire! I warn you!
Harry	And they'll shout back...

A chant starts.

Bessie	I don't know what you want from me.
Harry	So then it will start to get really savage.
George	You lot disperse!
Gil	Go to your own bloody homes!
Harry	Batons drawn, full on charges... police and soldiers trying to smash through a sheer wall of bodies...
Bessie	I don't know what you want.
Harry	Yes you do... yes you do... And I know it's what you want too. London... Paris... New York, Chicago, and you'll be the darling of 'em all... so long as you do... as I ask you.
Bessie	And if I say no?
Harry	I'll write back and tell Mr Leicester Square exactly how I met you...

Bessie	(*afraid*) You wouldn't.
Harry	Then there'll be mass panic... people screaming, trampling, scrambling to get away, save their lives, their own skin.
Bessie	Please Harry.
Gil	Hold the line!
Harry	I don't think he'll want you on at any of his theatres then.
Bessie	Please!
Harry	He could hardly have a lady of easy virtue up on the stage, never mind plying their trade in the cheap seats could he now.
Bessie	You wouldn't do that... to me?
Gil	Stay calm! Stand up!
Harry	And then... it'll happen.
Bessie	No!
Annie	George!
George	Stand together, defend the line all of you!
Annie	George! Stop it! Please!
Bessie	Harry! Stop it! Please!

Harry	Horses and men in the biggest scrum you'll ever see...
Bessie	(*crying*) What do you want from me?
Harry	You'll go before the Reverend's investigative panel my sweet... and you'll show him this...

Harry hands Bessie another letter.

It's the note Herbert gave to Lewy detailing exactly what he was offering... money, conditions, tenancy of the Red Lion.

Bessie	No! Never!
Gil	Hold together!
Harry	Oh yes. You'll say you found it... in Lewy's... bedroom.
Bessie	What if I put a match to it now? Then what?
George	Hold the line!
Harry	That's your choice... but know the cost. Do you want to lose all you dreamed of... for a Welsh pit lad, who wouldn't do as he was told?
Bessie	(*crying*) I hate you!
Harry	No you don't... I'm your one true friend... I love you Bessie... always have, always will... then... the soldiers'll raise their guns... first shots fired in the air... then into the crowd.

Bessie	You don't own me.
George	Get back in line all of you!! Stand up!!
Harry	But sooner or later some poor swine'll be stood in't wrong spot...
Gil	George! Get back!
Harry	And he'll stop a bullet
Bessie	I just want to be free of you!!

A shot rings out, George falls. For a moment we do not see or know who is shot.

Harry	Then they'll smash through, and push those mill gates wide open again. And all will be just as it should be.
Annie	George! No!
Bessie	(*weakly*) I hate you.
Harry	No you don't. You only think you do. I've got you what you always dreamed of Bessie. And it's only the start.

George is dead in the centre of the stage, Annie looks on grief stricken. Lewy, Gil and others look on.

SCENE 8

Herbert is alone when Lewy enters.

Lewy   Mr Dalton you didn't have to do that!

Herbert I had no choice. They were never going to yield. I tried to talk to him, you were there you saw it.

Lewy   George is dead.

Herbert Aye... I heard.

Lewy   Is that all you have to say? The man's dead!

Herbert What else is there to say? He shouldn't have been there.

Lewy   What? He was a friend of mine, I played alongside him. I went to his little un's christening. You don't give a stuff do you? We're just assets on a balance sheet to you aren't we? All this son this, lad that! We're like dray horses, if it goes lame shoot it and get another!

Herbert Now keep your damned head on and think straight!

Lewy   I am thinking straight! For the first time Mr Dalton!

Herbert Good. Then reckon up, I'm the only friend you have.

Lewy	Lucky me!
Herbert	Luck has got nothing to do with it. The reverend won't catch us, Stockwell knows where his bread's buttered, Gil won't dare turn on you, the people's hero, because they won't vote for him. We'll get through this… together… all you do is keep your trap shut and say nothing.
Lewy	I don't like it Mr Dalton… I don't like what I've seen, I don't know how I stand in church and square any of it I don't.
Herbert	Aye. We all have to stand before our maker one day Lewy. We'll have to hope he sees the good in us… why we did what we did. There's new coming… when we'll be free… to play and make money… to run our own game… free of the old school tie brigade… and trade unions too.

SCENE 9

The hearing re-forms. The Reverend now turns his attention to Harry.

Rev	Mr Stockwell, please allow me to welcome you to our Hearing. You have been involved with the West Broughton Club for some time, and though it may have been in a time when the rules were perhaps unclear, let this be an opportunity for you to make a clean breast of things. Do you have anything to offer us that may be of help in our enquiries?

Harry looks around the room. Lewy is nervous. The
Reverend confidently beams around the room, awaiting
Harry's evidence.

Harry   I'm afraid to say I do not Reverend.

Rev   I see. Are you absolutely certain of this?

Harry   I am.

Herbert grins widely at Lewy, winks at him in triumph.
Lewy breathes a huge and hearty sigh of relief.

Rev   Then it would seem that we have arrived at
               the end of the inquiry.

Harry turns his gaze to Bessie, who is white with stress,
anxiety. She shakes her head. He stares at her. This silent
play acts out as the Reverend speaks.

Rev   This is a very sad day for the game we all
               profess to love... I can only say that some
               individuals ought go from here and... hang
               their heads in shame. If there is one shred of
               decency within them they may at any time
               approach either me or the Rugby Football
               Union and make a statement, otherwise...

Bessie   I...

All stop, turn to look at Bessie.

Rev   I beg your pardon?

Lewy	Bess?
Bessie	I…
Herbert	She has nothing to add.
Rev	She can speak for herself.
Lewy	Bessie…?
Bessie	I'm sorry.
Lewy	What for?
Bessie	This. (*she holds out the piece of paper*) A note… I found it among Lewy's… things.
Lewy	No you didn't, I've never seen it.

The note is passed to the reverend. He reads it.

Rev	It details not only an initial payment of £100 upon signature, but a weekly payment of £2 for appearances, and confirms that the tenancy of the Red Lion Inn will also be secured and paid for.
Herbert	I never wrote anything of the like it's a forgery!
Rev	It is in your handwriting and is on your own headed notepaper! I think that in itself is proof!
Lewy	Bessie!?

Bessie   I'm sorry.

Herbert looks at her and then at Lewy.

Lewy   I never saw any note.

Rev   But you don't deny its contents?

Herbert   He does, everything.

Rev   Do you deny it!?

Lewy   I... I don't understand.

Rev   I do. The case is, by definition, proved. I'm
                afraid in view of this most serious breach of
                the amateur code I must pass the strongest
                sentence I am allowed, in my view wholly
                too lenient however. Mr Jenkins you are
                banned from the game of rugby football for
                two years.

Lewy   What?

Herbert   Two years!?

Bessie's head drops. Herbert is livid, Harry slyly
triumphant.

Rev   Were it within my power to impose a longer
                term I most definitely would. In addition
                West Broughton Rugby Club is also banned
                from playing any matches for a period of
                three months from this day.

Herbert	Your own club man!

Rev	Let it be known this verdict signals a determination to end the days of tawdry backhand deals. Furthermore know this, from this day on any club even suspected of paying a player shall be banned from playing or competing… on any level. This is the death knell for professionalism in the game of rugby… we should all celebrate. The game has been saved by the brave and honest testimony of Miss Butterworth, a young lady of the highest repute.

He gathers his papers and leaves. Staring in triumph at Lewy and Herbert as he goes, before exchanging a nod with Harry. Herbert turns on him.

Herbert	Stockwell… you're behind this you sly swine.

Harry	It's Mr Stockwell… and it's none of my doing… was it Bess? I'd take that seat on the board Herbert, but well, I've got bigger fish to fry. A seat on the Yorkshire RU committee. Not to mention dear old London, me and my Bessie. Bye bye Lewy, safe journey home son.

Harry exits.

Lewy	What now Mr Dalton?

Herbert pauses, then looks at him.

Herbert   You should have left that girl alone.

Herbert exits. Gil is the only one left with Lewy.

Gil   I told you. I tried to warn you all through.
               Don't get too thick with em... they don't care
               about us.

Gil exits too. Now only Lewy and Bessie remain. She makes
to go but he stops her.

Lewy   Tell me why! Why did you do it!?

Bessie   I had no choice. It's only 2 years, it'll pass,
               you'll be able to play again...

Lewy   All I want to know is why!? You, of all
               people?

He takes hold of her wrist.

Lewy   Why damn it!? Tell me! Harry made you do
               it... didn't he?

Bessie   Yes. The Empire Theatre Leicester Square
               that's why! I had no choice... alright!?

Lewy   He couldn't have stopped you going to
               London if that's what you wanted... I'd have
               gone with you.

Bessie   It's no good Lewy. The first time I worked in
               music halls... it was in the stalls and not on
               the stage.

Lewy	What? You were…?
Bessie	I was 15… Harry said I was too good to work at the bottom end of the scale, so he set me to work higher up. Proper gentlemen you know… not drunken colliers. Then one thing led to another… he brought me to live with him and said I could do a turn, see if I was any good at it. I always knew I would be… and I am. You see… I do love you… but there's only been one thing I wanted in my whole life Lewy… and I thought I could never get it… but now it's here… I'm sorry.
Lewy	And just when your dream arrives… he can take it away.
Bessie	I couldn't let him.
Lewy	You wouldn't have had to! We could have moved to London if that's what you wanted I'd have gone there.
Bessie	No good… Harry would have ruined it for me. He'd have told them where he found me… then what?
Lewy	You'd have me.
Bessie	Yes. And always be wondering… if I could have made it… like Marie Lloyd… now I'll be wondering the other way won't I? I'm sorry. You'll be able to play again… me… it was all or nothing.

Lewy	I'd have married you. Just shows what a fool I am doesn't it?
Bessie	Goodbye Lewy.

Bessie exits. Lewy is alone for a few seconds. He looks round to see a smiling Herbert. Lewy throws him a set of keys.

Lewy	Give them to Harry for me. I'd do it myself, but I don't want to be hung for murder, as well as playing rugby.
Herbert	Now son don't over react, it's all going to work out... but we have to box clever, cards close to the chest. There's changes coming, don't worry.
Lewy	I want no part of it.
Herbert	You're upset over the lass, bound to be, but there'll be another.
Lewy	Don't Mr Dalton! Just don't. Everything will work out for you won't it? One way, or the other. But me... I'm going home.
Herbert	Home? This is your home.
Lewy	No it's not. I was warned before I came... too stupid to listen.
Herbert	You'll feel different... in time. I'm sorry how things have gone.

Lewy	So am I. More than I knew I could be. Gil Gannon was right. All along.

Lewy exits. Herbert is alone. Across the stage the Reverend is equally alone, the catcalls slowly die down.

SCENE 10

Annie emerges, she has the baby with her, made from washing. She talks to the child and soothes it as she hangs washing out. She is disturbed by Herbert Dalton.

Annie	Oh… Mr Dalton.
Herbert	Hello Annie. Are you both well?
Annie	As we can be.
Herbert	How old is he now?
Annie	He's nearly two.
Herbert	Is he showing any aptitude with a rugby ball yet?
Annie	He's a strong little tyke, I know that. Gonna be tall as well, just like his dad.
Herbert	You know, I truly am sorry Annie.
Annie	What's past is past Mr Dalton. We go on. Because we have to. For this little feller… and for his dad too. I can forgive… but I don't want to forget.

Herbert	Nor should you. Nor should you. The Reverend is gone… people turned on him… banned their favourite player, banned his own club. No wonder they drove him out, they threw stones at him in the street.
Annie	He never understood this place… or the people. Still at least I can enjoy going to church again now.
Herbert	Aye. Well, there's a place for him on the team when he's old enough… by then it'll all be different.
Annie	But just the same… lads just wanting to play… girls taking a fancy to the lads that play… and everyone cheering of a Saturday… making heroes of 'em… money can't buy that.

He moves away from her, he is now joined by the entire ensemble, arranged as if around a large table.

SCENE 11

The brass band plays as all the ensemble don hats, and all take a cigar each and solemnly walk to their places. One stands up and speaks.

| Herbert | Gentlemen… good evening and thank you all for coming to the George Hotel tonight. It's a brave and a bold step we're taking. But one we can all be proud of. We're doing the right thing, taking our destiny in our hands… strong, confident in who we are, |

126

protecting our teams and towns... making sure our best young players can still play the game, and be a match for anyone, anywhere, and make us all proud.

Mills, factories, they come and go... and nobody will mourn them... but something we can all share... believe in...together... young and old... like this great game of ours... that will last forever, because it's the best of us, because it brings us all together. And it's bigger and more important than any of us. Let it be our legacy.

So, gentlemen it's become clear the game of Rugby cannot proceed in our areas along avowedly amateur lines. We therefore propose the following resolution: that the clubs here represented decide to form a Northern Rugby Football Union, and pledge themselves to push forward, without delay, its establishment on the principle of payment for bona fide broken time only. All in favour... say aye.

All   Aye.

Herbert   Gentlemen... to the future. The Northern
           Union.

All raise a glass and drink. Music comes in.

THE END

Mick Martin's agent: Christine Glover
Blake Friedmann,
1st Floor,
Selous House
5 – 12 Mandela St
London
NW1 0DU
Telephone: 0207 121 5964

NOTES

NOTES

NOTES

NOTES

NOTES

NOTES

NOTES

NOTES

NOTES

NOTES

NOTES

NOTES

NOTES

NOTES

NOTES

Discover our other titles and
stay up to date with all our latest releases at
www.scratchingshedpublishing.co.uk

www.TryReading.org

Public Libraries Supporting
Rugby League World Cup 2013
www.RLWC2013.com

The publication of this play script has been supported by
Try Reading, a partnership project of public libraries working
together to celebrate Rugby League World Cup 2013 and promote
reading and writing. Try Reading was a recipient of the National
Lottery supported Grants for the Arts Libraries Fund.